E-mail and News with Outlook Express

Books Available

By both authors:

BP327 DOS one step at a time
BP337 A Concise User's Guide to Lotus 1-2-3 for Windows
BP341 MS-DOS explained
BP346 Programming in Visual Basic for Windows
BP352 Excel 5 explained
BP362 Access one step at a time
BP387 Windows one step at a time
BP388 Why not personalise your PC
BP400 Windows 95 explained
BP406 MS Word 95 explained
BP407 Excel 95 explained
BP408 Access 95 one step at a time
BP409 MS Office 95 one step at a time
BP415 Using Netscape on the Internet*
BP420 E-mail on the Internet*
BP426 MS-Office 97 explained
BP428 MS-Word 97 explained
BP429 MS-Excel 97 explained
BP430 MS-Access 97 one step at a time
BP433 Your own Web site on the Internet
BP448 Lotus SmartSuite 97 explained
BP456 Windows 98 explained*
BP460 Using Microsoft Explorer 4 on the Internet*
BP464 E-mail and News with Outlook Express*
BP465 Lotus SmartSuite Millennium explained
BP471 Microsoft Office 2000 explained
BP472 Microsoft Word 2000 explained
BP473 Microsoft Excel 2000 explained
BP474 Microsoft Access 2000 explained
BP478 Microsoft Works 2000 explained

By Noel Kantaris:

BP258 Learning to Program in C
BP259 A Concise Introduction to UNIX*
BP284 Programming in QuickBASIC
BP325 A Concise User's Guide to Windows 3.1

E-mail and News with Outlook Express

by

P.R.M. Oliver
and
N. Kantaris

Bernard Babani (publishing) Ltd
The Grampians
Shepherds Bush Road
London W6 7NF
England

Please Note

Although every care has been taken with the production of this book to ensure that any projects, designs, modifications and/or programs, etc., contained herewith, operate in a correct and safe manner and also that any components specified are normally available in Great Britain, the Publishers and Author(s) do not accept responsibility in any way for the failure (including fault in design) of any project, design, modification or program to work correctly or to cause damage to any equipment that it may be connected to or used in conjunction with, or in respect of any other damage or injury that may be so caused, nor do the Publishers accept responsibility in any way for the failure to obtain specified components.

Notice is also given that if equipment that is still under warranty is modified in any way or used or connected with home-built equipment then that warranty may be void.

© 1999 BERNARD BABANI (publishing) LTD

First Published - March 1999
Revised Edition - February 2000

British Library Cataloguing in Publication Data:

A catalogue record for this book is available from the British Library

ISBN 0 85934 464 9

Cover Design by Gregor Arthur
Printed and Bound in Great Britain by Bath Press

About this Book

E-mail and News with Outlook Express has been written to help you get to grips with:

• Using e-mail to send and receive electronic messages.

• Finding your way round the thousands of Newsgroups available, and maybe finding something useful in them.

These days you can't read a paper, listen to the radio, or watch television very long before you hear or see mention of e-mail or the Internet. They have become an integral part of most of our lives over the last few years.

In this book an attempt has been made not to use too much 'jargon', but if some has crept in we are sorry. The book starts with a very short overview of the Internet and describes how e-mail and the Newsgroups fit into the general scene.

It then explains how you can obtain and install both Outlook Express 5 and Microsoft Explorer on your PC. How to go about connecting to the Internet is also very briefly covered. The book was written using version 5 of the Internet Explorer, working on one PC under Windows 98.

Chapters then follow on using Outlook Express 5 for handling all your e-mail and Newsgroup activities.

One thing to remember when reading the book is that the whole Internet scenario is changing every day, especially the World Wide Web. What is there to look at today, may have gone, or changed shape, by tomorrow, so we cannot guarantee that any Web references we give will still be the same when you come to view them.

The book does not describe how to set up your PC, or how to use Windows. If you need to know more about the Windows environment, then we suggest you select an appropriate book from the 'Books Available' list, which are all published by BERNARD BABANI (publishing) Ltd.

Like the rest of our computer series, this book was written with the busy person in mind. It is not necessary to learn all there is to know about a subject, when reading a few selected pages can usually do the same thing quite adequately. With this book, we hope that you will be able to come to terms with e-mail, the Newsgroups and Outlook Express 5, and get the most out of your computer in terms of efficiency, productivity and enjoyment, and that you will be able to do it in the shortest, most effective and informative way. Good luck.

If you would like to purchase a Companion Disc for any of our books listed on page ii, **apart from this book and the ones marked with an asterisk**, containing the file/program listings which appear in them, then fill in the form at the back of the book and send it to Phil Oliver at the address given.

About the Authors

Phil Oliver graduated in Mining Engineering at Camborne School of Mines in 1967 and since then has specialised in most aspects of surface mining technology, with a particular emphasis on computer related techniques. He has worked in Guyana, Canada, several Middle Eastern and Central Asian countries, South Africa and the United Kingdom, on such diverse projects as: the planning and management of bauxite, iron, gold and coal mines; rock excavation contracting in the UK; international mining equipment sales and international mine consulting. In 1988 he took up a lecturing position at Camborne School of Mines (part of Exeter University) in Surface Mining and Management. He retired from full-time lecturing in 1998, to spend more time consulting, writing, and developing Web sites.

Noel Kantaris graduated in Electrical Engineering at Bristol University and after spending three years in the Electronics Industry in London, took up a Tutorship in Physics at the University of Queensland. Research interests in Ionospheric Physics, led to the degrees of M.E. in Electronics and Ph.D. in Physics. On return to the UK, he took up a Post-Doctoral Research Fellowship in Radio Physics at the University of Leicester, and then in 1973 a lecturing position in Engineering at the Camborne School of Mines, Cornwall, (part of Exeter University), where between 1978 and 1997 he was also the CSM Computing Manager. At present he is IT Director of FFC Ltd.

Acknowledgements

We would like to thank both Microsoft for making this excellent software available free of charge, or commitment, on the Internet, and PC Plus for supplying it on the CD ROMs that appear with their magazine every month.

Trademarks

Arial and **Times New Roman** are registered trademarks of The Monotype Corporation plc.

HP and LaserJet are registered trademarks of Hewlett Packard Corporation.

IBM is a registered trademark of International Business Machines, Inc.

Intel is a registered trademark of Intel Corporation.

Microsoft, **MS-DOS**, **Windows**, **Windows NT**, and **Visual Basic**, are either registered trademarks or trademarks of Microsoft Corporation.

PostScript is a registered trademark of Adobe Systems Incorporated.

Macintosh, QuickTime and **TrueType** are registered trademarks of Apple Computer, Inc.

All other brand and product names used in the book are recognised as trademarks, or registered trademarks, of their respective companies.

Contents

1

Setting the Scene

What is E-mail

E-mail, or electronic mail, is a cheaper, quicker, and usually much easier way, to prepare and send messages than ordinary Post Office mail. So what is an e-mail? It is simply an electronic message sent between computers. These days it can also include attachments like pictures, document files, Web pages, or even pop songs. The message is passed from one computer to another as it travels through the Internet, with each node computer reading its e-mail address and routing it further until it reaches its destination, where it is stored in a 'mailbox'. This usually only takes a few minutes, and sometimes only seconds.

As long as you have a computer and can access the Internet you can use e-mail for keeping in touch with friends and family and for professional reasons. You can send e-mail to most people, anywhere in the world, as long as they have their own e-mail address. All Internet Service Providers, (ISPs), offer an e-mail address and mailbox facility to their customers. A mailbox, as its name suggests, is simply a storage area which holds your incoming messages until you are ready to look at them. Without this they would have nowhere to go whenever your own computer was switched off.

To retrieve your e-mail messages you have to contact your mailbox, download them to your PC, and then read and process them (just like any other mail).

There are many packages, some of them freely available, that make this whole procedure very easy, once you know how. One of our favourites is Outlook Express 5, which comes 'free' with Microsoft's Explorer 5 Web browser, which at the time of writing, was the most popular browser in use. If your PC has Windows 98 you will already have it; if not, we will point you in the right direction, but first we must set the scene.

What is the Internet? - A Brief History

The widespread use of e-mail has become possible because of the explosive growth of the Internet in the last decade, so how did this all come about?

In the mid 1960s with the cold war very prominent, the US military faced a strange strategic problem. How could the country successfully communicate after a possible nuclear war? They would need a command and control communication network linking the cities, states and military bases, etc. But, no matter how the network was protected it would always be vulnerable to the impact of a nuclear attack and if the network had a control centre it would be the first to go.

As a solution, the concept was developed that the network itself should be assumed to be unreliable at all times and should be designed to overcome this unreliability. To achieve this, all the nodes (devices attached to the network, which have their own address and use the network as a means of communication) would be equal in status, each with its own authority to originate, pass, and receive messages. The messages themselves would be divided into small parts, or packets, with each being separately addressed. The transmission of each packet of data would begin at a specified source node, and end at another specified destination node, but would find its own way through the network, with the route taken being unimportant. With this concept, if sections of the network were destroyed, that wouldn't matter as the packets would use the surviving parts.

The National Physical Laboratory, here in the UK, set up the first test network on these principles in 1968. Shortly afterwards, the Pentagon's Advanced Research Projects Agency (ARPA) funded a larger, more ambitious project in the USA, with the high-speed 'supercomputers' of the day as the network nodes.

In 1969, the first such node was installed in UCLA. By December of that year, there were four nodes on the infant network, which was named ARPANET, after its sponsor. The four computers could transfer data on dedicated high-speed transmission lines, and could be programmed remotely from the other nodes. For the first time, scientists and researchers could share one another's computer facilities from a long distance. By 1972 there were thirty-seven nodes in ARPANET.

The Origins of E-mail

It soon became apparent, however, that much of the traffic on ARPANET was not long-distance computing, but consisted of news and personal messages. Researchers were using ARPANET not only to collaborate on projects and to exchange ideas on work, but to socialise. They had their own personal accounts on the ARPANET computers, and their own personal addresses for electronic mail and they were very enthusiastic about this particular new service, which we shall hear much more of in the remainder of this book.

Throughout the 70s, the ARPA network grew, its decentralised structure making expansion easy as it could accommodate different types of computers, as long as they could speak the standard packet-switching language. ARPA's original standard for communication was known as NCP short for 'Network Control Protocol', but this was soon superseded by the higher-level standard known as TCP/IP, which has survived until today.

TCP, or 'Transmission Control Protocol', converts messages into streams of packets at the source, then reassembles them back into messages at the destination. IP, or 'Internet Protocol', handles the addressing.

Over the years, ARPANET itself became a smaller and smaller part of the growing proliferation of other networked machines, but TCP/IP linked them all. As the 70s and 80s advanced, many different groups found themselves in possession of powerful computers. It was fairly easy to link these computers to the growing global network. As the use of TCP/IP, which was in the public domain by that time, became more common, entire other networks were incorporated into the **Internet**.

In 1984 the National Science Foundation became involved and created the new NSFNET linking newer and faster supercomputers with bigger and faster links. Other US government agencies joined the bandwagon, including NASA, the National Institutes of Health and the Department of Energy.

ARPANET itself formally died in 1989, but its functions not only continued but were steadily improved. In Europe, major international 'backbone' networks started to provide connectivity to many millions of computers on a large number of other networks. Commercial network providers in both the US, Europe and Asia were beginning to offer Internet access and support on a competitive basis to any interested parties. In fact the extended use of the Internet cost the original founders little or nothing extra, since each new node was independent, and had to handle its own technical requirements and funding.

Now in the new century there are millions of nodes in the Internet, scattered throughout the world, with more coming on-line all the time and many more millions of people using this often named 'Information Super Highway' every day.

Built to be indestructible and with no centralised control, it's no wonder the word 'anarchistic' is often bandied around when the Internet is discussed!

Why Use the Internet?

Now we know what the Internet is, what can we use it for? Basically, five things spring to mind; two are the reason for this book, and the other three are mentioned briefly for completeness:

- Sending and receiving e-mail messages, the subject of this book.
- Taking part in News, or discussion groups.
- Accessing data stored on distant computers.
- Transferring data and program files from and to these distant computers.
- Browsing, or surfing the Net.

E-mail

Electronic mail, has to be one of the main uses of the Internet. It is very much faster that letter mail, which is known as 'snailmail' by regular e-mail users. It consists of electronic text, that is transmitted, sometimes in seconds, to anywhere else in the World that is connected to a main network. E-mail can also be used to send software and other types of files which are 'attached' to your message. As we shall see in later chapters, modern software such as Outlook Express makes this a very easy process.

Newsgroups

Discussion groups, or 'newsgroups', are another feature of the Internet that are easily accessed with Outlook Express. On the Internet they are generally known as USENET and consist of many, many thousands of separate groups which let you freely participate in discussions on a vast number of subjects.

Long Distance Computing

Using a program like Telnet you can maintain accounts on distant computers, run programs from them as if they were on your own PC, and generally make use of powerful supercomputers a continent away.

File Transfers

There is a fantastic amount of free software available over the Internet, as well as a multitude of text and graphic files of almost any subject you care to mention.

File transfers carried out with a protocol known as FTP, allow Internet users to access remote machines and retrieve these for their own use.

Surfing the Net

The World Wide Web, or Web as we shall call it, consists of client computers (yours and mine) and server computers which handle multimedia documents with 'hypertext' links built into them. Clicking the links on a page in a Web browser on your PC, brings documents located on a distant server to your screen, irrespective of the server's geographic location. Documents may contain text, images, sounds, movies, interactive programs (scripts), or a combination of these, in other words - multimedia. Surfing the Web just means moving from site to site and following the links that catch your eye.

Up until a year or two ago all of these activities required very expensive computing facilities and a large measure of computer literacy. Times have changed, however, and it is now possible for us 'non-geeks' to fairly easily and cheaply install a modem in our PC, connect to the Internet and with a Web browser, like Explorer (with comes with Outlook Express), carry them out with very little knowledge of what we are actually doing.

2

The Basic Requirements

To be able to use the e-mail and news facilities of Outlook Express you need a few basic items and skills.

Computer Hardware

First, you obviously need a computer! We have written this book with the current most common combination in mind - a PC running under Windows 95 or 98, but Microsoft has versions for other types of computers and for other operating systems. Most of our chapters will be equally useful if you use another version of Windows, a Macintosh, or even dare we say it, Linux, the PC variant of Unix.

If you buy a new PC, it will come with at least Windows 98 and with all the software we are concerned with here already installed. In this case you have no problems. Otherwise, the minimum hardware requirements to run the Windows 95 and NT versions of Explorer 5 and Outlook Express 5, are a 486DX/66 MHz, or higher, PC with 16 MB of RAM for Windows 95, 32 MB of RAM minimum for Windows NT (but as much RAM as possible is recommended). Between 70 MB and 111 MB of hard disc space will also be needed.

Ideally you will need a Pentium PC with as much RAM and hard disc space as you can get your hands on!

You also need a connection to the Internet, via a Modem, Ethernet Card, or ISDN direct digital phone line. A digital ISDN line is faster than a modem connection, but is considerably more expensive, at the moment.

Getting On Line

Unless you are lucky enough to have a PC which is connected to a Local Area Network (LAN) which has Internet access, you will need a modem to be able to communicate with the rest of the world. This is a device that converts data so that it can be transmitted over the telephone system.

You will also need to find, and possibly subscribe to, a suitable Internet Service Provider. There are many such providers in the UK. Most can be listed on the Web by accessing the following address:

http://thelist.internet.com/

and looking under the UK, or wherever else you are based. Another way would be to buy an Internet based PC magazine from your local newsagent and look at the reviews and adverts. Also you could try your friendly neighbourhood computer store, the telephone directory, or possibly adverts in the computer section of your local paper.

The present trend seems to be for new providers to give free Internet access and to pay for the service with advertising or other revenues. Be careful though before committing yourself to one provider as the quality of service can vary considerably. One thing we can't do here is make specific recommendations, but try and find someone who uses the company you decide on, or have a trial period with them.

What you are ideally looking for is **full dial-up SLIP or PPP connection with unlimited WWW access to the Internet**, and this should be possible by dialling a local number to your provider's access point. (SLIP and PPP are only two communication standards that you need to have, but do not need to understand).

The local call access will mean your phone bills should not be excessive, especially if you do your Internet accessing in off-peak times. The unlimited access means you will not pay any extra to your Internet Provider no matter how many hours you spend on line, just your monthly fee, if any.

A service, like that described, can cost in the region of £10 per month, but you can also get it free; there is a lot of competition.

From now on in this book, we assume that you have an active connection to the Internet. Trouble-shooting this is not within our remit!

Getting Your Software

If you already have your version of Explorer 5 and Outlook Express 5 up and running on your computer you can skip the rest of this section. If not, you may want to obtain the software. When you are actually connected to the Internet you can download Microsoft's Internet Explorer software absolutely free from their Web site at:

http://www.microsoft.com/windows/ie/default.htm

If you are not yet connected, you obviously can't do this, but there is a better way now anyway. Some computer magazines that come with CD-ROMs carry Web browsers on them. Our favourite is PC Plus, which includes, most months, the latest browsers from both Netscape and Microsoft. With the size of these browsers this can save many hours of valuable time downloading. The saving in your phone bill may well pay for the magazine as well. One thing to remember though with both sources is to select the version of Explorer designed for your operating system.

Installing Internet Explorer

If you have downloaded the program, simply double-clicking the downloaded .EXE program file from a Windows 95/98 or NT 'My Computer' window will start the installation procedure. From the CD-ROM just follow the instructions and click **Next** to continue. If you did not have enough space on your hard disc, you will be told to free up more room and try again. Good luck.

When you regain control of your PC, you may well find your desktop has changed somewhat. If you have any shortcut icons they will probably have been completely re-arranged, some new icons will have been added, and the Taskbar will have a Quick Launch bar like that with Windows 98, as shown below.

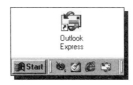

Here two new Outlook Express icons can be seen, one on the Desktop itself, and one on the Quick Launch bar. Clicking either of these will launch the program, as we shall see in the next chapter.

E-mail Addresses

Every e-mail user must have a unique address so that messages can be correctly routed to them. An e-mail address usually has two main parts, which are separated with the '@' character, and usually contain at least one dot (the '.' character). The following is a typical, if short, example.

aperson@organisation.co.uk

The part before the @ is the user name which identifies him, or her, at the mailbox. This user name is usually made up from the name and initials of the user, and must be unique on the mailbox server.

After the @ comes the domain name, which identifies the computer where the person has a mailbox and is often the name of a company, a university, or other organisation. There is a central register of these domain names, as each must be unique worldwide. When you set up your account, you can sometimes get your service provider to customise a domain name for you, at a price, of course. Otherwise you will probably use an extension of the domain name of the service provider itself.

Next, there's a '.' or dot, followed by two, or three, letters that indicate the type of domain it is. In our example above this is .co which means the host is a business or commercial enterprise, located in the United Kingdom (.uk). In the USA this could be .com instead, but not followed by a country identifier. A host name ending with .edu means the host is a US university or educational facility. A UK university would be .ac.uk. A .org indicates the host is a US non-commercial organisation.

Some of the more common extensions you might encounter are:

edu   Educational sites in the US

com   Commercial sites originally in the US, but now used for any such sites

gov   Government sites in the US

net   Network administrative organisations

mil   Military sites in the US

org   Organisations in the US that don't fit into other categories

fr   France

ca   Canada

uk   United Kingdom

Once you get used to these parts of addresses they begin to make more sense. For example, one of the writer's e-mail addresses is

poliver@csm.ex.ac.uk

This reads quite easily as:

P. Oliver located at Camborne School of Mines, part of the University of Exeter, which is an academic institution in the UK.

So if you know where somebody works you can even make an attempt to guess his, or her, e-mail address. A home address obtained through a commercial Internet provider would not be very easy though!

The E-mail Message

Before we get started with the Outlook Express program, perhaps a few words are in order about the actual content of electronic messages.

Message Headers

Most people will have used memos that have a series of headers at the beginning of the message text. They may look something like the following:

To:	Noel Kantaris
From:	Phil Oliver
Subject:	Microsoft Outlook Express 5
Date:	12 January 2000

E-mails have headers that are very similar and are essential for us so that we can see who a message is meant for, what it's about, who sent it, and when.

They have a more important use though, because as long as headers are consistently formatted, any e-mail program can easily sort out and present the messages received on a computer. It is this which allows users with different e-mail packages, with different types of computers, to send each other electronic messages.

The Body of the Message

Usually the body makes up the bulk of an e-mail message and looks very similar to any other word processed letter. Older e-mail programs were often limited to handling text in the ASCII character set, but the current generation allow elaborately formatted text and graphics, sound, and even multimedia video clips.

MIME Protocol

The use of multimedia was not possible with the original Simple Mail Transfer Protocol (SMTP - a very common e-mail protocol), so a new protocol, called MIME (Multi-purpose Internet Mail Extension) was developed, which allows you to include almost anything in an e-mail message.

As long as both you and your message recipient have MIME-enabled e-mail programs you can exchange any kind of multimedia file by simply appending it to your message. Outlook Express is MIME-enabled, but you should check to make sure that your recipient also has MIME, before sending them non-text attachments.

Free E-mail Services

As we saw earlier, the traditional way is to get your e-mail facilities from your Internet Service Provider, using a 'Pop 3' service to access a mailbox. A new trend is getting increasingly popular, at the moment, where free e-mail facilities are provided. With such schemes, once you are signed up, all your messages are stored on a Web page of a host computer, and to read or send your mail, you simply access that page with your Web browser. This way, all you need to handle your e-mail is access to the Web, and this can be from anywhere in the world. Privacy is provided with the usual user-name and password provisions.

There is something of a rush in the industry to provide such free facilities, the providers usually getting paid for carrying adverts on their sites. The more people that regularly access the sites to process their mail, the more the advertising revenue.

Apart from not costing anything, another advantage of these schemes is that you can keep the same e-mail address all the time, even if you change Service Providers.

Free accounts are at present available through most of the search engines (Yahoo, Hotbot, Excite, etc.), as well as BT and Microsoft Hotmail. One thing to watch though, is that not all free accounts support the use of attachments with your e-mails. We know that Excite and Hotmail do, but we have not tried out many more of them.

If you are on the move a lot, you may find this type of e-mail facility is better for you. You can send and receive your mail from any Internet linked computer, maybe at a friend's, in a hotel, or a 'Cyber Cafe'.

With Outlook Express 5 you can actually use Microsoft's Hotmail almost as if it was a Pop 3 mail account. You don't have to access your mail through a Web browser. This is quite an incentive to use that facility, and we have included a few pages on it in Chapter 5.

3

Outlook Express 5

Hopefully by now both Microsoft's Explorer 5 Web browser and Outlook Express 5 should have been installed on your system, if they were not already there. In this book we will not bother further with Explorer itself, but will concentrate on Outlook Express, the e-mail and news reader package that provides you with a very easy way to communicate electronically with the rest of the world.

Outlook Express

There are several ways to start the Outlook Express program; you can click the Desktop icon shown here, or the small icon on the left of the Windows Taskbar, shown in the last chapter.

With either method a window something like ours below should be opened.

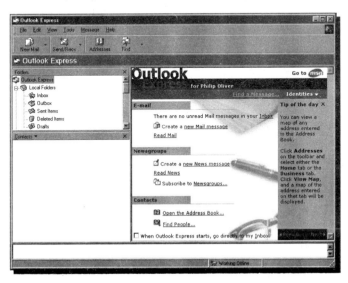

Connecting to your Server

Before you can use Outlook Express to send, or receive, mail you have to tell the program how to connect to your server's facilities. You do this by completing your personal e-mail connection details in the Internet Connection Wizard shown here, which usually opens when you first attempt to use the Read Mail facility.

The other way to enter this Wizard, if it does not open, or if you want to change your connection details, is to use the **Tools**, **Accounts** menu command, select the mail tab and click **Add**, followed by **Mail**.

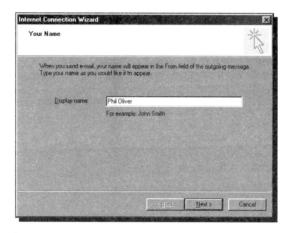

Type your name in the first box, as shown above, and click the **Next** button to open the second box. Enter your e-mail address in this box, if you have not organised one yet you could always check the **I'd like to sign up for a new account from Hotmail** option. Hotmail is a free browser based e-mail service now owned by Microsoft. Hence its inclusion!

In the third dialogue box enter your e-mail server details, as shown for us, on the next page. To complete some of the details here you may need to ask your Internet service provider, or system administrator, for help.

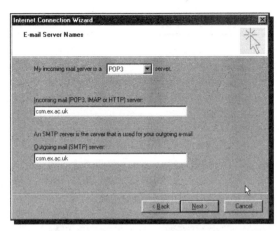

The details shown above will obviously only work for the writer, so please don't try them! In the next box enter your log-in name and password. Details of these should have been given to you by your Internet service provider or system administrator when you opened your 'service account'. You have now completed the Wizard so press **Finish** to return you to the Internet Accounts box, with your new account set up as shown below for us.

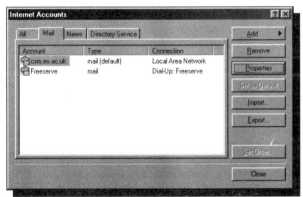

In the future, selecting the account in this box and clicking the **Properties** button will give you access to the settings sheets to check, or change, your details. We changed the Connection settings here to LAN (local area network).

The Screen Layout

The illustration below shows the main Outlook Express 5
window in Windows 98 with all the available bars and panes
showing.

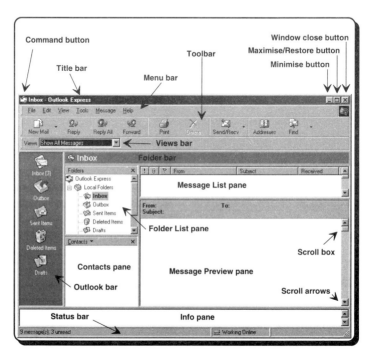

It is perhaps worth spending some time looking at the various
parts that make up this window, which is subdivided into
several areas with the following functions:

Area   *Function*
Command button   Clicking on this program icon button,
             located in the upper-left corner of
                    each window, displays the pull-down
                    Control menu which can be used to
                    control the window. It includes
                    commands for restoring, maximising,

	minimising, moving, sizing, and closing the window.
Title bar	The bar which displays the title of the current window.
Menu bar	The bar which allows you to choose from several menu options. Clicking on a menu item displays the pull-down menu associated with that item.
Minimise button	The button you point to and click to reduce the window, or application, to an icon on the Windows Taskbar.
Restore button	The button you point to and click to restore the window to its former size. When that happens, the Restore button changes to a Maximise button which is used to fill the screen with the active window.
Close button	The X button that you click to close the window.
Toolbar	A bar of icons that you click to carry out some of the more common program actions.
Scroll bars	If the contents of a window will not fit in it, scroll bars are added to the right and/or the bottom of the window.
Scroll arrows	The arrowheads at each end of a scroll bar which you can click to scroll the screen up and down, or left and right.
Scroll box	Dragging this box up, down, or across, the scroll bar will rapidly scroll through a message.

Views bar	Lets you choose which message views are displayed. By customising views you can see only the message you want to.
Outlook bar	An icon bar similar to Microsoft Outlook. Not really of much use.
Folder List	A list of icons for all the active mail folders, news servers and news-groups.
Message List	Shows a one line header for each message in the mail folder or newsgroup selected in the Folder List.
Contacts pane	Shows a list of names and addresses from the Address Book.
Preview pane	Shows the contents of the message selected in the Message List.
Status bar	The animated bar that shows the progress or status of the current operation.
Info pane	Shows extra information.

Note that when you move the mouse pointer over the tool or menu bars the selection 'lights up' to show that the feature is active.

You can control which of the above features display when you use Outlook Express from the Window Layout Properties dialogue box, opened with the **View**, **Layout** menu command. This box also lets you customise and control the display of the program Toolbars.

Menu Bar Options

Each option on the menu bar has associated with it a pull-down sub-menu. To access the menu, either click the mouse pointer on an option, or press the <Alt> key, which

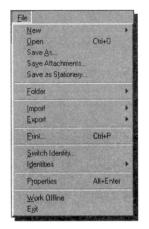

causes the first option of the menu (in this case **F**ile) to be highlighted, then use the arrow keys to highlight any of the options in the menu. Pressing either the <Enter> key, or the left mouse button, reveals the pull-down sub-menu of the highlighted menu option. The sub-menu of the **File** option is shown here.

Menu options can also be activated directly by pressing the <Alt> key followed by the underlined letter of the required option. Thus pressing <Alt+F>, also opens the sub-menu of **F**ile.

You can use the up and down arrow keys to move the highlighted bar up and down a sub-menu, or the right and left arrow keys to move along the options in the Menu bar. Pressing the <Enter> key selects the highlighted option or executes the highlighted command. Pressing the <Esc> key once, closes the pull-down sub-menu, while pressing the <Esc> key for a second time, closes the Menu system.

Note that those commands which are not available at any specific time will be inactive and appear on the menu in a lighter 'greyed out' colour.

Keyboard Shortcuts

Some of the menu options have keyboard shortcuts attached to them. These are very useful to people who are more used to the keyboard than the mouse. In the **File** sub-menu there are several. For example, pressing <Ctrl+P>, the 'P' key with the 'Ctrl' key also depressed, will start the printing procedure.

We have listed the available shortcuts in the Appendix.

Mouse Right-Click Menus

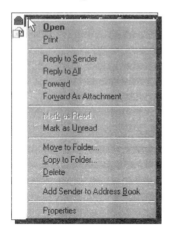

You can use your right mouse button to click objects in a window and see a drop-down shortcut, or context sensitive, menu, (the contents of which depend on what you click).

This example shows the options that were available when the mouse was right-clicked on a message header in the Message List pane.

The actions available were: Opening or printing the message; various ways of replying to, or forwarding the message, marking it as read, or as unread; moving or copying it to a folder, or deleting it; and adding the sender's details to your Address Book. Clicking on **Properties** would show details of the message file. As usual, unavailable options are shown in grey.

Toolbars

Most Windows applications are now fully equipped with Toolbar options, and Outlook Express is no exception. Each of its windows has its own Toolbar, with a series of icons, or buttons, that you can click with your mouse pointer to quickly carry out a program function. We give more details of these Toolbars as they are encountered, in the pages that follow.

That is enough background for now. In the next chapters we will work through the e-mail and news features of Outlook Express 5, and get you up and running as soon as possible.

4

E-mail with Outlook Express

Once your connection is established, you can click the Read
Mail coloured link, or the **Inbox** entry in the Folder List on the
left side of the Outlook Express 5 opening window. Both of
these actions open the Inbox, which when opened for the first
time, will probably contain a message from Microsoft, like
that shown below.

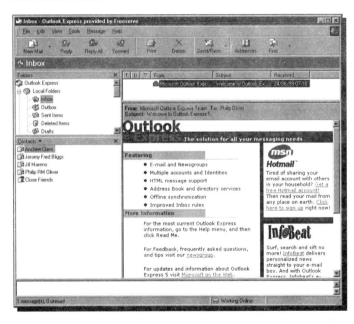

This shows the default Outlook Express Main window layout,
which consists of a Folder List to the left with a Contacts list
from the Address Book below it, a Message List to the right
and a Preview Pane below that. The Folder List contains all
the active mail folders, news servers and newsgroups.

Clicking on one of these places its contents in the Message List, and clicking on a message opens a Preview of it below for you to see. Double-clicking on a message opens the message in its own window.

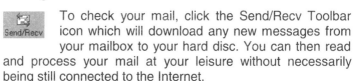 To check your mail, click the Send/Recv Toolbar icon which will download any new messages from your mailbox to your hard disc. You can then read and process your mail at your leisure without necessarily being still connected to the Internet.

A Trial Run

Before explaining in more detail the main features of Outlook Express we will step through the procedure of sending a very simple e-mail message. The best way to test out any unfamiliar e-mail features is to send a test message to your own e-mail address. This saves wasting somebody else's time, and the message can be very quickly checked to see the results.

 Click the New Mail icon and select **No Stationery** to open the New Message window, shown above.

Type your own e-mail address in the **To:** field, and a title for the message in the **Subject:** field. The text in this subject field will form a header for the message when it is received, so it helps to show in a few words what the message is about. Type your message and when you are happy with it, click the Send toolbar icon.

By default, your mesage is stored in an Outbox folder, and pressing the Send/Recv Toolbar icon will send it, hopefully straight into your mailbox. When Outlook Express next checks for mail, it will find the message and download it into the Inbox folder, for you to read and enjoy!

The Main Window

After the initial opening window, Outlook Express uses three other main windows, which we will refer to as; the Main window which opens next; the Read Message window for reading your mail; and the New Message window, to compose your outgoing mail messages.

The Main window consists of a Toolbar, a menu, and five panes with the default display shown in our example on page 18. You can choose different pane layouts, and customise the Toolbar, with the **View**, **Layout** menu command, but we will let you try these for yourself.

The Folders List

The folders pane contains a list of your mail folders, your news servers and any newsgroups you have subscribed to. There are always at least five mail folders, as shown in our example on the next page. You can add your own with the **File**, **Folder**, **New** menu command from the Main window. We added 'My new folder' like this. You can delete them again with the **File**, **Folder**, **Delete** command. These operations can also be carried out after right-clicking a folder in the list. You can drag messages from the Message List and drop them into any of the folders, to 'store' them there.

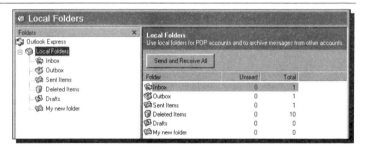

Note the icons shown above, any new folders you add will have the same icon as that of our added one above.

The Contacts Pane

This pane simply lists the contacts held in your Address Book. Double-clicking on an entry in this list opens a New Message window with the message already addressed to that person.

The Message List

When you select a folder, by clicking it in the Folders list, the Message list shows the contents of that folder. Brief details of each message are displayed on one line.

The first column shows the message priority, if any, the second shows whether the message has an attachment, and the third shows whether the message has been 'flagged'. All

of these are indicated by icons on the message line, like our example to the left. The 'From' column shows the message status icon (listed on the next page) and the name of the sender, 'Subject' shows the title of each mail message, and 'Received' shows the date it reached you. You can control what columns display in this pane with the **View**, **Columns** menu command.

To sort a list of messages, you can click the mouse pointer in the title of the column you want the list sorted on, clicking it again will sort it in reverse order. The sorted column is shown with a triangle mark.

Message Status Icons

This icon	Indicates this
0	The message has one or more files attached.
!	The message has been marked high priority by the sender.
↓	The message has been marked low priority by the sender.
⊠	The message has been read. The message heading appears in light type.
⊠	The message has not been read. The message heading appears in bold type.
⊠	The message has been replied to.
⊠	The message has been forwarded.
⊡	The message is in progress in the Drafts folder.
⊠	The message is digitally signed and unopened.
⊠	The message is encrypted and unopened.
⊠	The message is digitally signed, encrypted and unopened.
⊠	The message is digitally signed and has been opened.
⊠	The message is encrypted and has been opened.
⊠	The message is digitally signed and encrypted, and has been opened.
⊞	The message has responses that are collapsed. Click the icon to show all the responses (expand the conversation).
⊟	The message and all of its responses are expanded. Click the icon to hide all the responses (collapse the conversation).
▽	The unread message header is on an IMAP server.
✗	The opened message is marked for deletion on an IMAP server.
▼	The message is flagged.
↓	The IMAP message is marked to be downloaded.
⊞↓	The IMAP message and all conversations are marked to be downloaded.
⊟↓	The individual IMAP message (without conversations) is marked to be downloaded.

The Preview Pane

When you select a message in the Message list, by clicking it once, it is displayed in the Preview pane, which takes up the rest of the window. This lets you read the first few lines to see if the message is worth bothering with. If so, double clicking the header, in the Message list, will open the message in the Read Message window, as shown later in the chapter.

You could use the Preview pane to read all your mail, especially if your messages are all on the short side, but it is easier to process them from the Read Message window.

The Main Window Toolbar

 Opens the New Message window for creating a new mail message, with the To: field blank.

 Opens the New Message window for replying to the current mail message, with the To: field pre-addressed to the original sender. The original Subject field is prefixed with Re:.

 Opens the New Message window for replying to the current mail message, with the To: field pre-addressed to all that received copies of the original message. The original Subject field is prefixed with Re:.

 Opens the New Message window for forwarding the current mail message. The To: field is blank. The original Subject field is prefixed with Fw:.

 Prints the selected message.

 Deletes the currently selected message and places it in the Deleted Items folder.

 Connects to the mailbox server and downloads waiting messages, which it places in the Inbox folder. Sends any messages waiting in the Outbox folder.

 Opens the Address Book.

 Finds a message or an e-mail address using Find People facilities of the Address Book.

The Read Message Window

If you double-click a message in the Message list of the Main window the Read Message window is opened, as shown below.

This is the best window to read your mail in. It has its own menu system and Toolbar, which lets you rapidly process and move between the messages in a folder.

The Read Message Toolbar

This window has its own Toolbar, but only two icons are different from those in the Main window.

Previous - Displays the previous mail message in the Read Message window. The button appears depressed if there are no previous messages.

Next - Displays the next mail message in the Read Message window. The button appears depressed if there are no more messages.

Viewing File Attachments

Until fairly recently, e-mail on the Internet was good only for short text notes. You couldn't send attachments like formatted document or graphic files with your messages. That changed with the advent of MIME, which stands for Multipurpose Internet Mail Extension. With Outlook Express you can send Web pages, other formatted documents, photos, sound and video files as attachments to your main e-mail message, and some of them as part of the actual message itself.

One thing to be careful of though, is to make sure that the person you are sending your message to has e-mail software capable of decoding them. In our experience many people seem to stick to their tried and trusted 'old' e-mail software that does not.

A file attachment appears at the bottom of the message in the Read Message window. To save the attachment, use the **File**, **Save Attachments** menu command, or right-click the attachment and select the **Save As** option.

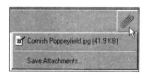

To display, or run, an attachment from the preview pane, click the paper-clip file attachment icon in the preview pane header, and then click the file name. You may get a virus warning here, but if you are happy about the document source just carry on. To save the attachment click the **Save Attachments** button that is opened, as shown above.

The New Message Window

We briefly looked into the New Message window earlier in the chapter. This is the window, shown next, that you will use to create any messages you want to send electronically from Outlook Express. It is important to understand its features, so that you can get the most out of it.

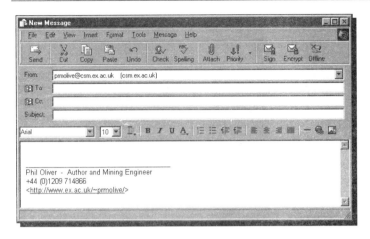

As we saw, this window can be opened by using the New Mail Toolbar icon from the Main window, as well as the **Message**, **New Message** menu command. From other windows you can also use the **Message**, **New** command, or the <Ctrl+N> keyboard shortcut. The newly opened window has its own menu system and Toolbar, which let you rapidly prepare and send your new e-mail messages.

Message Stationery

Another Outlook Express feature is that it lets you send your messages on pre-formatted stationery for added effect, as in our example on the next page.

To access these, click the down arrow next to the New Mail button in the Main window and either select from the **1** to **10** list, as shown here, or use the **Select Stationery** command to open a box with many more stationery types on offer.

To send a plain message, with no 'fancy' effects, use the **No Stationery** option.

Dear friends,

Happy Christmas from all in Cornwall

Phil Oliver - Author and Mining Engineer
+44 (0)1209 714866
< http://www.ex.ac.uk/~prmolive/ >

The New Message Toolbar

 Send Message - Sends message, either to the recipient, or to the Outbox folder.

 Cut - Cuts selected text to the Windows clipboard.

 Copy - Copies selected text to the Windows clipboard.

 Paste - Pastes the contents of the Windows clipboard into the current message.

 Undo - Undoes the last editing action.

 Check Names - Checks that names match your entries in the address book, or are in correct e-mail address format.

Spelling - Checks the spelling of the current message before it is sent.

 Attach File - Opens the Insert Attachment window for you to select a file to be attached to the current message.

 Set Priority - Sets the message priority as high or low, to indicate its importance to the recipient.

 Digitally sign message - Add a digital signature to the message to confirm to the recipient that it is from you.

 Encrypt message - Encodes the message so that only the recipient can read it.

 Work Offline - Closes connection to the Internet so that you can process your mail offline. The button then changes to **Work Online.**

Your Own Signature

If you have created a signature from the Main window in the **Tools**, **Options**, **Signature** tabbed box, as shown at the top of the next page, its text is automatically placed for you at the end of the message creation area.

You could also create a more fancy signature file in a text editor like Notepad, or WordPad, including the text and characters you want added to all your messages, and point to it in the **File** section of this box. We have chosen to **Add signatures to all outgoing messages**, but you could leave this option blank and use the **Insert**, **Signature** command from the New Message window menu system if you prefer.

Message Formatting

Outlook Express provides quite sophisticated formatting options for an e-mail editor from both the **Format** menu and Toolbar. These only work if you prepare the message in HTML format, as used in Web documents. In the **Tools**, **Options**, **Send** box you can set this to be your default mail sending format.

To use the format for the current message only, select **Rich Text (HTML)** from the **Format** menu, as we have done here. If **Plain Text** is selected, the black dot will be placed against this option on the menu, and the formatting features will not then be available.

The above Format Toolbar is added to the New Message window when you are in HTML mode and all the **Format** menu options are then made active.

All of the formatting features are well covered elsewhere in the book so we will not repeat them now. Most of them are quite well demonstrated in Microsoft's opening message to you. You should be able to prepare some very easily readable e-mail messages with these features, but remember that not everyone will be able to read the work in the way that you spent hours creating. Only e-mail programs that support MIME (Multipurpose Internet Mail Extensions) can read HTML formatting. When your recipient's e-mail program does not read HTML, the message appears as plain text with an HTML file attached.

At the risk of being called boring we think it is usually better to stick to plain text, not only can everyone read it, but it is much quicker to transmit and use.

Adding Attachments

If you want to send a Web page, or other type of file as an attachment to your main e-mail message you simply click the Insert File Toolbar button and select the file to attach. This opens the Insert Attachment dialogue box, for you to select the file, or files, you want to go with your message.

The attached files are shown in a special 'Attach:' section in the message header, as shown below.

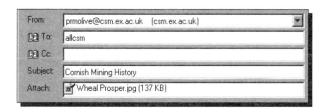

Sending E-mail Messages

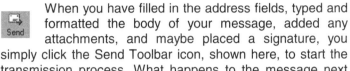 When you have filled in the address fields, typed and formatted the body of your message, added any attachments, and maybe placed a signature, you simply click the Send Toolbar icon, shown here, to start the transmission process. What happens to the message next depends on your settings.

If you have a dial-up connection (using a modem) you may want to keep the message and transmit it later, maybe with several others to save on your telephone bill. In that case, make sure the **Send messages immediately** option is not selected in the **Tools**, **Options**, **Send** settings box. Clicking the above Send Toolbar icon will then place the message in the Outbox folder.

When you are ready to send your held messages you click the Send/Recv Toolbar icon on the Main window. If you forget to do this, Outlook Express will prompt you with a message box when you attempt to exit the program.

When the **Send messages immediately** option is selected, your messages will be sent on their way as soon as you click the Send Toolbar button. This option is best used if you have a permanent connection to the Internet, or your e-mail is being sent over an internal network, or Intranet.

Replying to a Message

When you receive an e-mail message that you want to reply to, Outlook Express makes it very easy to do. The reply address and the new message subject fields are both added automatically for you. Also, by default, the original message is quoted in the reply window for you to edit as required.

With the message you want to reply to still open, either click the Reply to Sender Toolbar icon, use the **Message**, **Reply to Sender** menu command, or use the <Ctrl+R> keyboard shortcut. All these actions open the New Message window and the message you are replying to will, by default, be placed under the insertion point.

With long messages, you should not leave all of the original text in your reply. This can be bad practice, which rapidly makes new messages very large and time consuming to download. You should usually edit the quoted text, so that it is obvious what you are referring to. One or two lines may even be enough.

Removing Deleted Messages

Whenever you delete a message it is actually moved to the Deleted Items folder. If ignored, this folder gets bigger and bigger over time, so you need to check it every few days and manually re-delete messages you are sure you will not need again, in which case you are given a last warning message.

If you are confident that you will not need this safety net, you can opt to **Empty messages from the 'Deleted Items' folder on exit** in the **Tools**, **Options**, **Maintenance** settings box, opened from the Main window. You will then have a short time to change your mind before they are finally deleted.

Organising Your Messages

Perhaps most of the e-mail messages you get will have no 'long term' value and will be simply deleted once you have dealt with them. Some however you may well need to keep for future reference. After a few weeks it can be surprising how many of these messages can accumulate. If you don't do something with them they seem to take over and slow the whole process down. That is the reason for the Folders List.

As we saw earlier you can open and close new folders in this area, and can move and copy messages from one folder into another.

To move a message, you just select its header line in the Message List and with the left mouse button depressed 'drag' it to the folder in the Folders List, as shown to the left. When you release the mouse button, the message will be moved to that folder.

The copy procedure is very much the same, except you must also have the <Ctrl> key depressed when you release the mouse button. You can tell which operation is taking place by looking at the mouse pointer. It will show a '+' when copying, as on the right.

The System Folders

Outlook Express has five folders which it always keeps intact and will not let you delete. Some of these we have met already.

The *Inbox* holds all incoming messages. You should delete or move messages from this folder as soon as you have read them.

The *Outbox* holds messages that have been prepared but not yet transmitted. As soon as the messages are sent they are automatically removed to the *Sent Items* folder. You can then decide whether to 'file' your copies of these messages, or whether to delete them. As we saw on the last page, any messages you do delete are placed in the *Deleted Items* folder as a safety feature.

The last system folder is the *Drafts* folder, which does not seem to be mentioned at all in Microsoft's program information. If you close a message without sending it, Outlook Express will ask you to save it in this folder. We also use the Drafts folder to store our message pro-formas and unfinished messages that will need more work before they can be sent.

5

Some Other Features

Outlook Express Help

Outlook Express has a built-in Help system, which is accessed with the **Help**, **Contents and Index** menu command, or the **F1** function key. These open a Windows 98 type Help window, as shown below.

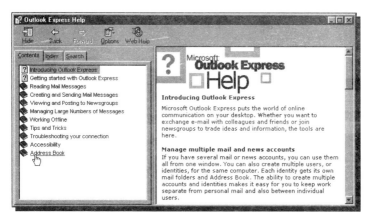

We strongly recommend that you work your way through all the items listed in the **Contents** tabbed section. Clicking on a closed book icon will open it and display a listing of its contents. Double-clicking on a list item will then open a window with a few lines of Help information.

Another way of browsing the Help system is to click the **Index** tab and work your way through the alphabetic listing. The **Search** tab opens a search facility you can use, as shown next. In this example we typed 'check spelling' in the **Type in the keyword to find** text field and clicked the **List**

Topics button. Then, selecting one of the **Topic**s found and clicking **Display**, opened Help information on it, with the words searched-for highlighted, as shown below.

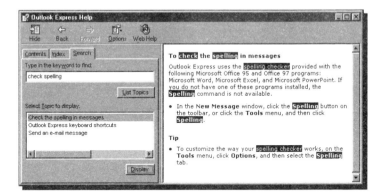

If you want to copy any of the text displayed, you will first have to use the **Options**, **Search Highlight Off** command, then select the text you want, right-click it, and select **Copy** from the opened menu. If you are connected, the Web Help icon accesses the Support Online from Microsoft Technical Support which can give more specific help with the program, though we have not tried it.

The Help provided by Microsoft with Outlook Express 5, is a big improvement over some earlier versions, and it is well worth spending an hour or two getting to grips with it. There still seem to be some glaring omissions though!

Spell Checking

Many of the e-mail messages we receive seem to be full of errors and spelling mistakes. Some people do not seem to read their work before clicking the 'Send' button. With Outlook Express this should be a thing of the past, as the program is linked to the spell checker that comes with other Microsoft programs. If you do not have any of these, the option will not be available to you, though.

To try it out, prepare a message in the New Message window, but make an obvious spelling mistake, maybe like ours below. Pressing the Spelling Toolbar button, the **F7** function key, or using the **Tools**, **Spelling** command, will start the process.

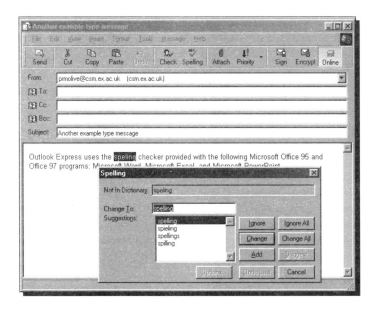

Any words not recognised by the checker will be flagged up as above. If you are happy with the word just click one of the **Ignore** buttons, if not, you can type a correction in the **Change To** field, or accept one of the **Suggestions**, and then click the **Change** button. With us the **Options** button always seemed 'greyed out', but you can get some control over the spell checker on the settings sheet opened from the main Outlook Express menu with the **Tools**, **Options** command, and then clicking the **Spelling** tab.

The available options, as shown on the next page, are self explanatory so we will not dwell on them. If you want every message to be checked before it is sent, make sure you select the **Always check spelling before sending** option.

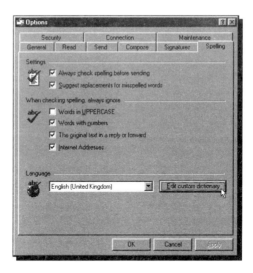

Connection at Start-Up

While you are looking at the program settings, open the **Tools**, **Options**, **Connection** tabbed sheet, shown below. This gives you some control of what happens when you open Outlook Express, depending on your connection settings for Internet Explorer. If you have a modem connection to the Internet, it can be annoying when a program goes into dial-up mode unexpectedly.

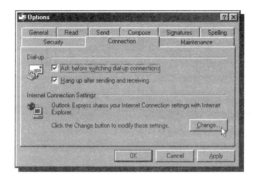

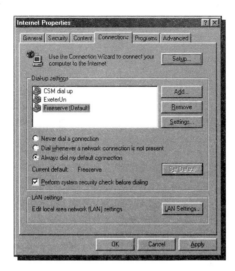

As it stands above we would be connected to our 'Freeserve' mailbox whenever we started Outlook Express. With a permanent Internet connection this would be fine, but with a modem connection, we prefer to have the above **Never dial a connection** option selected. Then when we are ready to 'go on line', as long as we have not selected **Work Offline** as a **File** menu option, we simply click the Send/Recv toolbar icon shown here. If you have more than one Internet connection, the down arrow to the right of the icon lets you select which one to use.

Printing your Messages

It was originally thought by some, that computers would lead to the paperless office. That has certainly not proved to be correct. It seems that however good our electronic communication media becomes most people want to see the results printed on paper. As far as books are concerned, long may that last!

Outlook Express 5 lets you print e-mail messages to paper, but it does not give you any control over the page settings it uses. You can, however, alter the font size of your printed output as it depends on the font size you set for viewing your messages. As shown here, you have five 'relative' size options available from the **View**, **Text Size** menu command.

When you are ready to print a message in the Read Message window, use the <Ctrl+P> key combination, or the **File**, **Print** menu command, to open the Print dialogue box shown below.

Make sure the correct printer **Name** and **Properties** are selected, choose the pages to be printed, how many copies you want, and finally click **OK** to start the printing process. You can also click the Print toolbar icon shown here to start the printing procedure.

If the message has Web page links on it, there are two features in the above dialogue box, as when printing from the Internet Explorer browser:

• The **Print table of links** option, which when checked, gives a hard copy listing of the URL addresses of all the links present in the page.

• The **Print all linked documents** option, which not only prints the message, but all the Web pages linked to it.

The Address Book

E-mail addresses are often quite complicated and not at all easy to remember. With Outlook Express there is a very useful Address Book built in and an almost empty example of one is shown here.

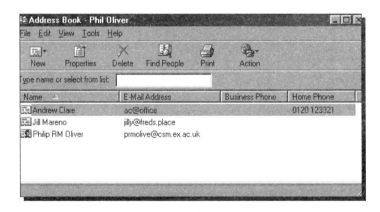

It can be opened from the Main window by clicking the Address Book Toolbar icon, or using the **Tools**, **Address Book** menu command.

Once in the Address Book, you can manually add a person's full details and e-mail address, in the Properties box that opens when you click the New Toolbar icon and select **New Contact**, as shown here. Selecting **New Group** from this drop-down menu lets you create a grouping of e-mail addresses, you can then send mail to everyone in the group with one operation.

To send a new message to anyone listed in your Address Book, open a New Message window and use the **Tools**, **Select Recipients** command, or click on any of the To, Cc, or Bcc icons shown here on the right.

In the Select Recipients box which is opened, you can select a person's name and click either the **To:->** button to place it in the **To:** field of your message, the **Cc->** button to place it in the **Cc:** field, or the **Bcc->**button to place it in the **Bcc:** field.

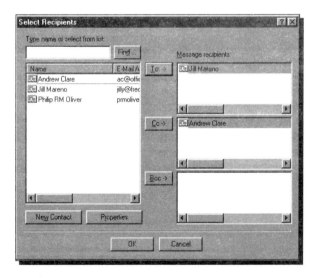

The **New Contact** button lets you add details for a new person to the Address Book, and the **Properties** button lets you edit an existing entry, as shown on the facing page.

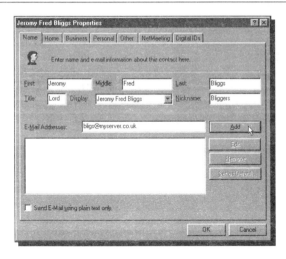

Address Book Help

We will leave it to you to find your way round this very comprehensive facility. Don't forget that it has its own Help system that you can use with the **Help**, **Contents and Index** menu command. An example section is shown open below.

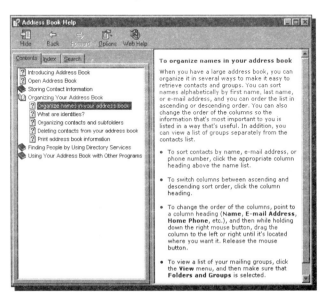

Using Message Rules

If you are ever in the situation of receiving e-mail messages from a source you do not want to hear from, you can use Message Rules to filter your incoming messages. Unwanted ones can be placed in your Deleted Items folder straight away. It can also be useful for sorting incoming messages and automatically routing them to their correct folders.

To open this feature, which is shown below, use the **Tools**, **Message Rules**, **Mail** menu command and select the criteria you want your incoming messages to be processed by.

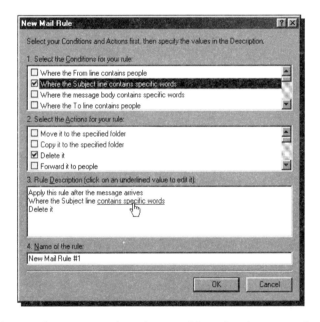

In box 1 above, you select the conditions for the new rule. In box 2 you control what actions are taken, and the new rule itself is automatically 'built' for you in box 3. If you use this feature much you will probably want to name each of your rules in box 4.

In our example on the previous page, we have set to intercept and delete messages which contain certain words in their Subject Lines. To complete the rule we clicked on the 'contains specific words' link and filled in the following dialogue box.

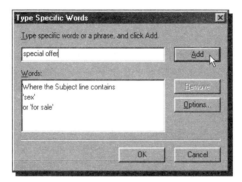

When finished clicking on **OK** twice opens the Message Rules box shown below.

In this box you can control your rules. You can set multiple rules for incoming messages and control the priority that messages are sorted in the list. The higher up a multiple list a condition is the higher will be its priority.

If an incoming message matches more than one rule, then it is sorted according to the first rule it matches in your list.

Blocked Senders List

With Outlook Express 5 there is a very easy way to prevent messages from a problem source ever disturbing your peace again. When you first receive such a message, select it in the Messages List and action the **Message**, **Block Sender** menu command, as we did in the example below.

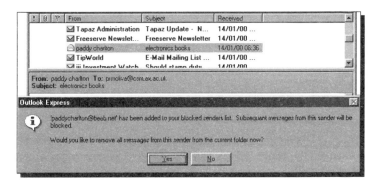

This can be a very powerful tool, be careful how you use it!

The **Message**, **Create Rule from Message** menu command is a quick way to start the New Rule process, as the details of the currently selected message are automatically placed in the New Mail Rule box for you.

People that send mass junk mailings often buy lists of e-mail addresses and once you are on a list you can be sure that your mailbox will never be empty again! With these tools at your disposal you should only ever receive 'junk mail' once from any particular source.

Microsoft Hotmail

As we saw at the end of Chapter 2, if you don't have a mail account with an Internet Service Provider you can always use one of the free HTTP (Hypertext Transfer Protocol) services like Hotmail, where your messages are stored on a server. Using it you can access your e-mail from any computer with an Internet connection, anywhere in the world.

You have to be live to sign up with Hotmail, so you may have to do it from work, or a friend's PC, or a Cyber Cafe. From the Main Outlook Express window use the **Tools**, **New Account Signup** command and select **Hotmail** (with us it was the only option anyway), to open the following box.

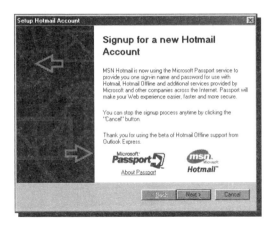

This was the first of eight boxes in our case. You have to complete each one before the **Next** button will let you proceed. None of them were particularly onerous, and after about only twenty minutes we were registered, as follows.

Clicking the **Finish** button (not shown on our example) completes the procedure, and a new Folder icon should be added to the Folders List, as shown here.

The first time you click the new Hotmail icon it downloads several standard Hotmail folders for you to use.

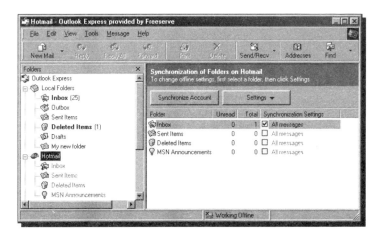

If you look carefully in the Folders List above, you can see that the entries in the Hotmail section are a lighter grey, this is because the folders are actually stored on a distant server, not on your PC.

Having a server-based account allows you to save time by downloading only your message headers so that you can choose which messages you want to later download and view in their entirety.

When you work 'offline', using the **File**, **Work Offline** menu command, you can read and respond to your e-mail messages just as you would when working online. The next time you go online, maybe by clicking the **Synchronize Account** button shown above, your server-based mail account will synchronise the mail on your computer with the server. During this process, the actions you performed in your account will be duplicated on the server.

Mailing Lists

When you start using e-mail you will probably want to receive lots of messages, but until your friends get active there is often a lull. This may be the time to join a mailing list.

Mailing lists are automatic mailing systems where a message sent to a list address is automatically sent on to all the other members of the list. The programs that manage this automatic mailing have names like Listserv, or Majordomo, which usually form part of the List address. Some of these lists are moderated and work much like journals, where submissions are accepted, sometimes edited, and then forwarded to subscribers. Others, however, have no constraints put on their contents! Although the quality and quantity vary from list to list, you can often find a wealth of free information in them.

To subscribe to a list, you need to know the name of the list and its address. Commands can vary between different lists, but they often follow the format given below. Note that there is a difference between the address to which you send postings, or messages, for the list, and the address you use for subscribing to it. Be sure to distinguish between these two addresses. One of the most common mistakes made by new Internet users is to send subscription requests to list addresses, which are then forwarded to all the members on the list. Please don't make this mistake, it can be annoying and time consuming for other list readers.

Finding a Suitable List

There are literally thousands of Mailing lists which you can join, covering almost every subject imaginable, from science, to art, to hobbies, and of course to any type of kinky sex. One of the biggest problems is finding the ones for you. Fortunately, there are several Web sites which give details of Mailing lists. A good one we have used, with lists grouped by topic should be found at:

http://wwwneosoft.com/internet/paml/subjects

This will put you in direct contact with your selected lists, where you will get instructions on how to subscribe and proceed. Make sure you keep a copy of any instructions, you will need them in the future, if you want to unsubscribe, or change your subscription details.

Typical Subscription Commands

All of these commands go to the subscription address:

sub *listname First Last*   To subscribe to *listname*, with your *First* and *Last* names given.

signoff *listname*   To unsubscribe from a list.

set *listname* **nomail**   To turn off mail from a list if you are going away.

set *listname* **mail**   To turn the mail back on when you return.

Once you have mastered Mailing lists you need never have an empty mailbox again. In fact you may find them to be a little overpowering, but lists can be a wonderful source of up to date information.

Often Used E-mail Symbols

Once you start receiving messages from lists and other places around the globe, you may encounter some of the following acronyms, and symbols, which people often use to relieve the general boredom of life.

Acronyms

Btw	By the way
cu	See you (bye)
Faq	Frequently asked question
fyi	For your information
imho	In my humble opinion
imo	In my opinion
Rotfl	Rolling on the floor laughing
rtfm	Read the manual!
Ttyl	Talk to you later

Smileys

You tilt your head sideways to see them:

:-)	Smiling
:-D	Laughing
;-)	Winking
:-O	Surprise
:-(	Frowning, Sad
:-I	Indifferent
:-/	Perplexed
:-{)	Smiley with a moustache
8-)	Smiley with glasses
<:-I	Dunce
:-X	My lips are sealed
:->	Sarcastic

If these appeal to you, you can get a more comprehensive selection from the *Unofficial Smiley Dictionary* reached at the following Web address:

http://www.eff.org/papers/eegtti/eeg_286.html#SEC287

6

News with Outlook Express

Discussion groups, or 'newsgroups', are a main feature of the Internet and are easily accessed with Outlook Express. They are often known as Usenet groups and consist of many thousands of separate news groups which let you actively take part in discussion on a vast number of topics. In fact almost any subject you could think of is covered, and the number of groups is growing larger all the time.

Outlook Express is a program you can use for viewing, and posting (or mailing), messages to these Usenet groups. Unlike e-mail, which is usually 'one-to-one', newsgroups could be said to be 'one-to-many'.

How Usenet Works

Usenet messages are shipped around the world, from host system to host system, using one of several available protocols, that you don't need to bother too much about. Your host server stores all of its Usenet messages in one place, which everybody with an account on the system can access, if they want. That way, no matter how many people actually read a given message, each host has to store only one copy of it. The host systems contact each other regularly and bring themselves up to date with the latest Usenet messages, sometimes this happens thousands of times a day.

Usenet is huge. We once saw it quoted that every day Usenet users transmit over 60 million characters into the system. Some of this information has to be of use! In fact there are so many active groups now, it is unlikely that your server will handle more than a fraction of them. This can be frustrating, if you keep seeing references to a group that you cannot access through your server.

Usenet Newsgroups

The basic building block of Usenet as we have seen is the newsgroup, which is a collection of messages with a related theme. These are arranged in a particular hierarchy that originated in the early 80s. Newsgroup names start with one of a series of broad topic names. For example, newsgroups beginning with 'sci' should have scientific and engineering content. These broad topics are followed by a series of more specific topic names. '**sci.engr**' groups, for example, are limited to discussion about engineering subjects, and '**sci.engr.mining**' would be a group dedicated to very specific discussion on mining engineering topics.

There are many national and regional groups, including **uk**, but some of the main topic headers are:

alt	Controversial, sexual, and unusual topics; not always carried by servers.
bionet	Research biology.
bit.listserv	Conferences originating as Bitnet mailing lists.
biz	Business.
comp	Computers and related subjects.
misc	Discussions that don't fit anywhere else.
news	News about Usenet and its groups.
rec	Hobbies, games and recreation.
sci	Science and engineering, other than research biology.
soc	Social groups, often ethnically related.
talk	Politics and related topics.

With such an almost unlimited choice, you should very soon be able to subscribe to your own unique reading list of newsgroups. Subscribing does not mean you have to pay something, but means that when you enter News you will only see the groups in which you are most interested, and won't have to search through all of the others every time.

Starting to Read News

Initially you can start the News process from the opening window of Outlook Express 5, by clicking the 'Subscribe to Newsgroups' link as shown below.

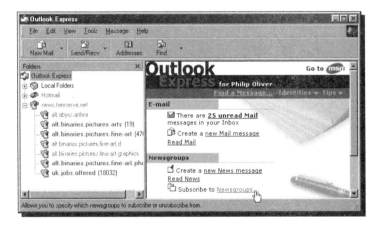

When first used, this opens the Internet Connection Wizard for you to complete your details. Once this has been completed and you have subscribed to one, or more, newsgroups, you simply click on a newsgroup folder in the Folders List to access that newsgroup. Our example above shows seven newsgroups and one news server in the list.

Internet News Configuration

Before you can access the Usenet groups you must make sure that your details and those of your news server are entered into the Internet Connection Wizard. If necessary, you can open this from the **Tools**, **Accounts**, **News** settings box by clicking the **Add** button and then selecting **News**.

Complete the details in the dialogue boxes as they are presented, entering the server name in the **Ne<u>w</u>s (NNTP) server** field, as shown here.

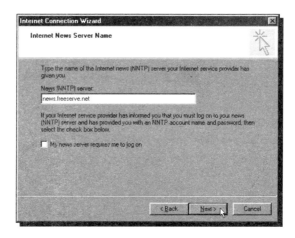

If this is a closed, or members only type server, then complete the log-on details which you should have been given. Otherwise keep clicking **Next** until finally the program starts downloading the server groups. Be warned the whole procedure can take well over half an hour.

As can be seen in many of our examples, we use Freeserve as one of our Internet Service Providers. This service is free and available to anyone that registers, so you should have no problem following our examples if you want to. Freeserve's News service has about 35,000 newsgroups, which is nowhere near complete. To get 'all' of the groups, especially the more exciting 'alt' ones, you would probably have to register with one of the remaining pay services. Hence the saying 'You get what you pays for..'

There are also hundreds of open news servers on the Internet that allow you to connect to them without a password. You should be able to find lists of them by searching for 'open news servers' with one of the search engines. Open news servers do not often stay permanently available though.

The Newsgroup Subscriptions Window

The initial set-up procedure finishes by downloading a list of all the groups available on the news server. As there are well over 35,000 available to some servers this can take quite a while. When this is done, a window similar to ours below opens and you can see what newsgroups are available to you. If you are subscribed to more than one server, the **Newsgroups** pane lists the groups available from the server selected in the **Account(s)** pane.

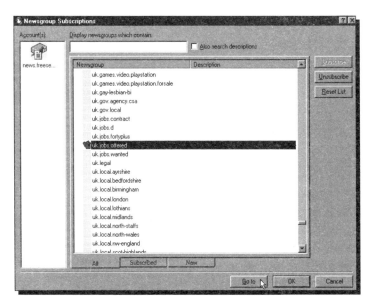

If you scroll down through the list of groups, almost at the bottom you should find some that start with **uk**. In our example, we selected **uk.jobs.offered** and clicked the **Go to** button, which is an easy way to have a look at the contents of a group. An easier way would have been to type 'uk.jobs' into the **Display newsgroups which contain** field. Only the seven that matched this criterion would then have displayed.

A one line header (for each of the first 300 of the 18,032 messages contained in the group that day), was loaded into the Message Header pane, as shown below. Not too much unemployment in the computer industry these days!

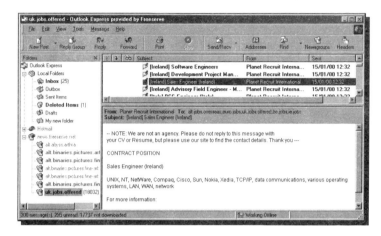

As soon as one of these headers is selected, the message itself appears in the Preview pane below it. This can take a few moments, don't forget it has to be downloaded over the network from your server.

Subscribing to a Group

If you think a group looks interesting and would be useful in the future, you should subscribe to it. To do this, re-open the Newsgroup Subscriptions window by clicking the Newsgroups Toolbar button, highlight the group and click the **Subscribe** button. A newspaper icon is placed alongside the group name in the listing. To remove a group from your subscribed list, you simply select it and click the **Unsubscribe** button.

Once you have selected all the groups you regularly want to keep tabs on, click the **Subscribed** tab button at the bottom of the list. In the future, each time you open the Newsgroups window, it will only display your chosen list. At any time while this window is open you can click **All** to see a complete listing again, or **New** to see any new groups.

The News Window

The News window, shown on the facing page, is almost the same as the Main e-mail window. It contains three panes, a Folders List, a Message Header List, and a Preview pane.

Clicking on a Newsgroup in the Folders List, displays a listing of that group's current headers in the Message Header List, which by default has seven columns:

🔘	Message has file(s) attached.
⬇	Message is marked for offline viewing.
👓	Watch/ignore this conversation.
Subject	Shows the subject line of the message.
From	Gives the 'name' of the sender of the news message.
Sent	States the date and time the message was posted to the group.
Size	Gives the size of the file in KB.

You can sort messages by any of these columns and in ascending or descending order, by clicking in the column header. You can also add, remove, or rearrange the columns, and sort them, with the **View**, **Columns** menu command.

Clicking on a message header, when you are on-line, downloads and displays the message body text in the Preview pane.

The News Toolbar

Opens a New Message window for creating a new e-mail message, with the To: field blank.

Opens the New Message window for sending a message to be posted in the currently selected newsgroup.

Opens the New Message window for replying privately to the sender of the current news message, with the To: field pre-addressed to the original sender.

Opens the New Message window for forwarding the current news message. The To: field is blank. The original Subject field is prefixed with Fw:.

Prints the current message.

Stops the current downloading operation. This option is only available when the download Status Indicator in the top right corner of the window is rotating.

Attempts to make a dial-up connection and downloads selected messages or headers, as well as updating any e-mail folders and sending any waiting messages.

Opens the Outlook Express Address Book.

Lets you search for messages, text, or for people's e-mail details.

Opens the Newsgroup Subscriptions window in which you select which news server to use and the groups subscribed to.

Downloads new headers for the selected group from the server, in batches of 300.

The Read Message Window

Double-clicking on a message header in the News window, opens a Read Message window with the message in it, as shown below.

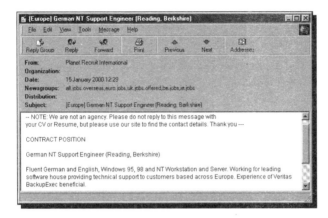

This window has its own menu and Toolbar, and moving the mouse pointer over a Toolbar button shows what the button's action will be. Apart from the three icons described below, this window is very much the same as the e-mail Read Message window described in an earlier chapter.

Replying to Messages

As long as you have chosen to make Outlook Express your default news reader in the **Tools**, **Options**, **General** settings box, the News window Toolbar icons will use the Mail facilities to easily send messages of three different types.

 The **Reply to Group** icon addresses your message to the current newsgroup for all to read.

 The **Reply to Sender** icon addresses an e-mail message to the individual who posted the current news message.

The **Forward** icon prepares an e-mail with a copy of the current message, for you to address and complete.

Be very careful not to mix these up, the result could be embarrassing if you post a very personal message to the whole group, for maybe millions of people to read!

Postings Containing Pictures

If you have time to explore the many thousands of **alt** groups, you will find that a lot of them contain messages with picture files attached that are (or should be) relevant to the group name. Our example below shows one being downloaded from a group that does not normally need censoring, but be warned, many of them do these days! You never really know what you will find in them.

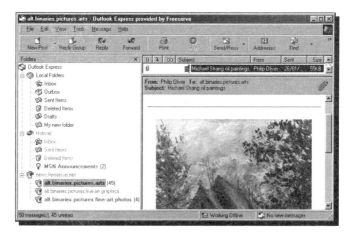

Clicking a message in the Header Pane will, as long as you are connected, download the message body in the Preview pane, and you will be able to view any graphics in the message, as shown above. When the image file has been completely downloaded, you can use the **File**, **Save Attachments** command to save any images in it to your hard disc.

Usually a paper clip icon is placed on the title bar of the Preview pane, as with e-mail attachments. Clicking this icon will show the name of the attached file and give you the option to **Save Attachments**.

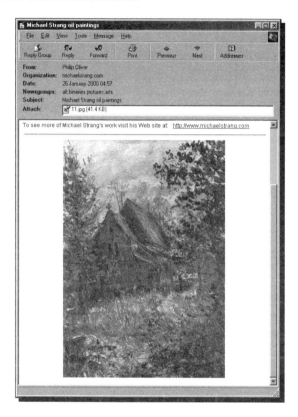

The same message with the whole example of excellent English contemporary art is shown above, but this time opened in its own Read Message window, by double-clicking the message header. The image attachment is shown in its own **Attach** box below the message headers.

To view, or run other message attachments, double-click their icons. As before, to save a file attachment, use the **File**, **Save Attachments** menu command, or right-click the attachment and select the **Save Picture As** option.

Threaded Messages

When a message is placed on a newsgroup, often someone replies and then a 'thread' or 'conversation' is formed.

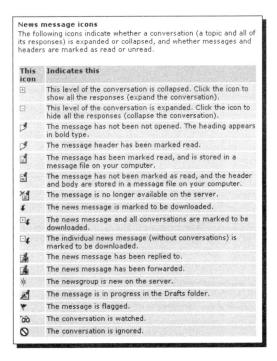

The edited News Help window above shows how you can recognise the status of any news messages in the Message Header list of a News window. Outlook Express messages are not threaded by default, but you can change this by checking the **Automatically expand grouped messages** option in the **Tools**, **Options**, **Read** settings sheet. Message replies would then always be placed with the original messages.

If you want the message list to display only the original message in a thread (conversation), select the first message, and then use the **View**, **Collapse** menu command, or click the minus (-) sign next to the original message.

Off-Line Viewing

If, like most of us, you are usually busy and don't have time to wait for long newsgroup messages to be downloaded, you can synchronise your accounts, or set up a batch download process, and view selected headers or whole messages off-line later on.

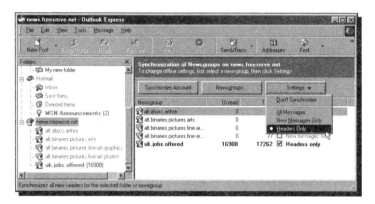

In the Main window in Offline mode, select one or more newsgroups you subscribe to whose messages you want to read offline. Click the **Settings** button, and then select the option you want from the drop-down menu, as shown above. This marks the group with what you want transferred from the server to your computer during synchronisation.

All Messages	Download all messages on the server to your computer.
New Messages Only	Download only messages that are new to the server since you last synchronised.
Headers Only	Download only headers with details of message subject, author, date, and size.

Whenever you want to transfer the messages or headers to your computer from the server, click the **Synchronize Account** button and go and make a cup of coffee.

A downloading box, similar to the one above, will show you
how the download process is going. You can click the
Details button to see more information about what is
happening. If you are using a modem connection, you should
definitely check the **Hang up when finished** option. Your
phone bill will almost certainly be big enough already!

After you download messages for off-line reading and
have disconnected from the Internet, you can return to the
News Window and the message header icons, shown on
Page 68, will show the status of any saved, or cached,
headers or messages. Clicking the **View**, **Current View**,
Show Downloaded Messages menu command, will display
only the downloaded messages for you to read. Have fun.

Newsgroup Caches

Each newsgroup you subscribe to has its own cache file on
your computer and everything you download from that group,
either manually or for off-line viewing, is saved in this cache.
When you select to view an item that is stored in a cache it is
'instantly' displayed, as it does not have to be downloaded.
This is all very well, but if you are not careful you can fill your
hard disc up with material you don't even know you are
keeping.

Controlling the Caches

The **Tools**, **Options**, **Maintenance** settings sheet gives you
control of the size of all your cached message files when you
click the **Clean Up Now** button.

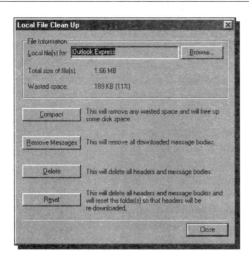

Here you can manually compact, delete, or remove messages from all or specific message files, newsgroups, or servers, including Hotmail. You access all these 'local' files on your PC by clicking the **B**rowse button.

This clean-up procedure is usually known as 'purging'. Some of these 'manual clean up' options are also available from the News menu with the **File**, **Folder** command.

Purging unused, old, or large newsgroups can increase your free hard disc space enormously. Most news servers remove old messages and headers on a regular basis, sometimes even weekly. The next time you connect to a newsgroup you've purged, your cache is rebuilt with just the current messages and headers from the server.

Some Internet Etiquette

Often called 'netiquette' the following list, we once found[1], although somewhat stilted makes good reading and should help you avoid upsetting too many people on the Net:

1   DON'T include the entire contents of a previous posting in your reply.

   DO cut mercilessly. Leave just enough to indicate what you're responding to. NEVER include mail headers except maybe the 'From:' line. If you can't figure out how to delete lines in your mailer software, paraphrase or re-type the quoted material.

2   DON'T reply to a point in a message without quoting or paraphrasing what you're responding to.

   DO quote (briefly) or paraphrase. If the original 'Subject:' line was 'Big dogs' make sure yours says 'Re: Big dogs'. Some REPLY functions do this automatically. By net convention, included lines are preceded by '>' (greater-than signs).

3   DON'T send lines longer than 70 characters. This is a kindness to folks with terminal-based mail editors. Some mail gateways truncate extra characters turning your deathless prose into gibberish.

   Some mail editor tools only SEEM to insert line breaks for you, but actually don't, so that every paragraph is one immense line. Learn what your mail editor does.

4   DON'T SEND A MESSAGE IN ALL CAPS. CAPITALISED MESSAGES ARE HARDER TO READ THAN LOWER CASE OR MIXED CASE.

---

[1]   Patrick Crispen's Internet Roadmap

DO use normal capitalisation. Separate your paragraphs with blank lines. Make your message inviting to your potential readers.

5   DON'T betray confidences. It is all too easy to quote a personal message and regret it.

DO read the 'To:' and 'Cc:' lines in your message before you send it. Are you SURE you want the mail to go there?

6   DON'T make statements which can be interpreted as official positions of your organisation, or of offers to do business.

DO treat every post as though you were sending a copy to your boss, your minister, and your worst enemy.

7   DON'T rely on the ability of your readers to tell the difference between serious statements and satire, or sarcasm. It's hard to write funny. It's even harder to write satire.

DO remember that no one can hear your tone of voice. Use smileys, like:

:-) or **:->**

turn your head anti-clockwise to see the smile.

You can also use capitals for emphasis, or use Net conventions for italics and underlines as in: "You said the guitar solo on "Comfortably Numb" from Pink Floyd's, The Wall, was *lame*? Are you OUT OF YOUR MIND???!!!"

8   DON'T send a message that says nothing but "Me, too", or something equally as trivial. This is most annoying when combined with (1) or (2) above.

On Your Own

You should, by now, have enough basic knowledge to happily venture forth into the unknown.

Good luck, but please remember that there are millions of other newsgroup readers, and you never know where, or who, they are. Please watch what you say, or include, in your postings, there is enough rubbish there already.

Appendix

Keyboard Shortcuts

Keyboard shortcuts for Outlook Express

Shortcut	Action
Shortcut	*Action*
General	
F1	Open help topics
Ctrl+A	Select all messages
Main Mail Window	
Ctrl+O	Open the selected message
Ctrl+Q	Mark a message as read
Tab	Move between window panes
Main and Read Mail Message Windows	
Sh+Ctrl+B	Open the Address Book
Ctrl+D	Delete a message
Ctrl+F	Forward a message
Ctrl+I	Go to your Inbox
Ctrl+M	Send and receive mail
Ctrl+N	Open a new message
Ctrl+P	Print the selected message
Ctrl+R	Reply to the message author
Sh+Ctrl+R	Reply to all
Ctrl+U	Go to next unread message
Ctrl+Y	Go to folder
Ctrl++	Go to next message in the list
Ctrl+<	Go to previous message in the list
Alt+Enter	View properties of selected message

Mail New Message Window

F3	Find text
F7	Check spelling
Esc	Close a message
Ctrl+K	Check names
Ctrl+Enter	Send a message
Sh+Ctrl+S	Add a signature

Main News Window

Sh+Ctrl+A	Mark all news messages as read
Ctrl+J	Go to next unread newsgroup
Sh+Ctrl+M	Download news for off-line reading
Ctrl+O	Open the selected message
Ctrl+Q	Mark a message as read
Ctrl+W	Go to a newsgroup
Ctrl+Y	Go to a folder
Tab	Move between window panes
← or +	Expand a news thread
→ or -	Collapse a news thread

Main and Read News Message Windows

F5	Refresh headers and articles
Ctrl+F	Forward a message
Ctrl+G	Reply to all
Ctrl+N	Post new message to the newsgroup
Ctrl+P	Print the selected message
Ctrl+R	Reply to the author
Ctrl+Sh+U	Go to next unread thread
Ctrl+>	Go to the next message in the list
Ctrl+<	Go to previous message in the list
Alt+Enter	View properties of selected message

News New Message Window

Sh+Ctrl+F	Find text
Esc	Close a message
Ctrl+K	Check names
Alt+S	Send a message
F7	Check spelling

Index

Companion Discs

COMPANION DISCS are available for most computer books written by the same author(s) and published by BERNARD BABANI (publishing) LTD, as listed at the front of this book (except for those marked with an asterisk).

There is no Companion Disc for this book

To obtain companion discs for other books, fill in the order form below, or a copy of it, enclose a cheque (payable to **P.R.M. Oliver**) or a postal order, and send it to the address given below. **Make sure you fill in your name and address** and specify the book number and title in your order.

Book No.	Book Name	Unit Price	Total Price
BP		£3.50	
BP		£3.50	
BP		£3.50	
Name .... Address		Sub-total	£............
		P & P (@ 45p/disc)	£............
		Total Due	£............
Send to: P.R.M. Oliver, CSM, Pool, Redruth, Cornwall, TR15 3SE			

PLEASE NOTE

The author(s) are fully responsible for providing this Companion Disc service. The publishers of this book accept no responsibility for the supply, quality, or magnetic contents of the disc, or in respect of any damage, or injury that might be suffered or caused by its use.

TRUST

CYAN|CAMPUS

TRUST
THE BEST WAY TO MANAGE

REINHARD K. SPRENGER

TRANSLATED BY GRAHAM LINKER

First published in German as *Vertrauen führt: Worauf es im Unternehmen wirklich ankommt* by Campus Verlag, Frankfurt/Main, 2002

This translation first published in Great Britain in 2004 by Cyan/Campus Books, an imprint of

Cyan Communications Limited
4.3 The Ziggurat
60–66 Saffron Hill
London EC1N 8QX
www.cyanbooks.com

A CIP record for this book is available from the British Library

ISBN 0-9542829-8-1

Printed and bound in Great Britain by
TJ International, Padstow, Cornwall

CONTENTS

INTRODUCTION

"I will now put down my weapons.
Then we can talk to each other."

Chief Inspector Stephan Derrick from the popular German detective series *Derrick*

Do you trust your staff? Do your staff trust you? How do you know? (My trust is limited, you see.) Do you trust your boss? In what way? Does he keep you informed? Does he refrain from looking over your shoulder all the time? Or is it just that he hasn't fired you? Or were you thinking of all these things at the same time?

In this book, I advocate trust. I argue for more trust between superiors and staff and between colleagues and partners. I make the case for trusting trust and mistrusting mistrust. I can see the difficulties inherent in trusting people, but I also know that the advantages of a culture of trust outweigh the disadvantages. Trust is safer than any safety measure. Trust is a more effective control than any control system. Trust creates more value than any value-creation initiative.

Before I begin to explain my case, I'd like to give a brief explanation of the background to this book. In a way, it represents the culmination of a train of thought and writing.

In my 1991 book *Mythos Motivation* [The Motivation Myth], I described the mechanism of bonus systems and incentives as institutionalized mistrust. "I don't believe you are willing to work!" "I don't regard you as a partner capable of entering into an agreement!" These messages take people's motivation and throw it back in their faces. This is why so many management systems fail; they are really saying "I don't trust you!"

Later, in *Das Prinzip Selbstverantwortung* [The Self-Confidence Principle], published in 1995, I introduced a constructive alternative. The focus here was the member of staff himself: the quality of his state of mind as he goes to work in the morning, his self-motivation and commitment. What do people need in order to work in a committed way on their own initiative? I looked at self-management as an inner attitude that facilitates a high level of performance on a long-term basis. The final chapter of the book outlined the concept of credibility, thereby describing an aspect of trust but without making it the central theme.

Then, in 2000, came *Aufstand des Individuums* [Revolt of the Individual]. Here I highlighted the major structural shortcomings in companies that hinder the success factors for the future: commitment, innovation and entrepreneurial spirit. In the second part of the book, under the heading "The individualizing company," I presented a management concept in which I repeatedly touched on the issue of trust as the basis for effective co-operation, although I never treated it directly as a subject.

After the book was published, I couldn't let go of trust. I sensed that something of great importance hadn't yet been said, and that new territory was waiting for me. You may find this irritating; after all, the term "trust" has been bandied around in management for a long time. Indeed, I don't know any business manager who doesn't consider trust to be the most important factor in staff management. I don't know any speaker who doesn't preach trust as the key to a value-oriented corporate culture. I don't know of any serious book on management that doesn't look at the potential economic benefits of trust. And yet I have never met anyone who has explained to me what trust is.

It was Alan Fox in 1974 who proclaimed the "high-trust culture" to be a competitive advantage. Not much has happened since then, not least because although Fox mentions trust as an explanation for co-operative behaviour, he doesn't treat it as a *phenomenon that itself needs to be explained*. It is used as *explanans* (the thing that gives an explanation) but not as *explanandum* (the thing to be explained). And these two have about as much in common as pecans and canned peas.

In companies, trust remains a word that puts the person to whom it is said (who evidently does not trust) in a very bad light: vain, smug and fishing for compliments. Trust is most frequently invoked when something important isn't working in the company. It is usually senior managers who broach the subject from on high in a demanding way: people ought to and they should, and if they don't, then....

This apart, it is only the new idealistic literature that deals with trust. We find material about trust everywhere. It can no longer be heard, read and taken seriously in the traditional sense; instead it surrounds us like a fog of exhaust fumes. This material doesn't try to bring about agreement by means of an argument. Instead it presumes agreement by using the term "trust" as a formula for consensus. People consign all their hopes and longings to this linguistic passe-partout. Open your mouth and swallow! *We* have understood, it's just the spoilsports who don't really want to do it. Such optimistic appeals are not wrong, just meaningless. Few books and articles that mention trust in the title get beyond moralistic murmurings, demands for transparency and a pointless "It would be great if..." In short, a lot of hot air printed on paper.

So what *is* trust? Is it a feeling? A moral stance? A quaint idea from the good old days? A trendy term from corporate phraseology? A problem-solving cliché? A rhetorical trick that clever people use as a smokescreen for their power plays? An article of faith?

A weasel word that follows us around in our working life like flies following a cow?

Not even the academic disciplines offer us a reliable shoulder to lean on. There hasn't yet been any agreement on a common definition of trust. And yet I have been helped by other people's works, which I mention in the bibliography. Without Tanja Ripperger's excellent dissertation, I wouldn't have been able to write this book in the way I did. The anthology published by Martin Hartmann and Claus Offe, as well as Niklas Luhmann's monograph – for a long time the only one that existed – have left unmistakable traces.

We can see the yawning gulf between the need for trust and the rhetoric about it on the one hand, and real action on the other. Putting conviction into practice just doesn't happen. Is this because management only pays lip service to trust? Or are the inherent difficulties to blame? Can nothing be done? Is trust always to be the unattainable holy grail?

If you are a manager from the old school, you might reply "Trust? It's a load of hot air. Facts and data, that's what I need. Don't talk to me about gut feelings. It doesn't get us anywhere." Trust stands there like a chapel between two skyscrapers. It lacks rationality. It has overtones of home, closeness and co-operation, and promises security and something beyond the present, but offers no tangible economic benefit. It defies common sense: too naïve, too mysterious, too nostalgic.

But what if it turned out that some goods that are necessary in business could be won only through trust? What if future economic survival depended on these goods? What if trust could be proved to be a hard factor, one that pays off? Not an entry on the balance sheet or a financial performance figure, but something that plays an important role in the whole company and affects its operating result? Wouldn't we be stupid to ignore it?

Trust is fascinating because it is linked to so many aspects of commercial life: agreement, reciprocity, co-operation, contracts, management, speed, innovation, reliability and commitment. And it is one of the main management tools in a company, alongside power and money. This is precisely where my reflections begin. In real life, trust starts where there is no substitute for it. Let's take a closer look. Everyone can see that power and money no longer work in the way they did for decades. The economic framework has changed. Structural changes have weakened power and money as management instruments of flexible organizations with a decentralized structure. In any case, they were only the result of failed trust. We didn't resort to these methods until we were let down.

So I am going to explain why trust is the subject of the future. Globalized fast markets, flexible working patterns, virtual forms of organization – this is the way the economy seems to be going. For many companies, it is already a reality. That's why the need for trust has increased dramatically. On the other hand, it is these very conditions that pose a massive threat to trust in business life. The old and commonly held view of trust, which is based on the assumption that the circumstances of life will remain constant, must inevitably be invalidated by modern business conditions. We are now seeing a difference whose consequences we haven't even begun to understand. The philosopher Peter Sloterdijk says that tomorrow's society is condemned to trust.

There is another factor: the most important distinction in modern business is no longer between labour and capital, or between entrepreneur and consumer, or between state and market – that's all nineteenth-century stuff. No, the most important distinction is between creditors and debtors: what a creditor believes of a debtor and what this belief costs. The taker asks himself: "Am I prepared to get into debt because I trust my productivity?" The giver asks: "Do I trust that the money will come back?" Trust is thus at the core of the modern economy. You don't need any great powers of prediction to see this: trust will be the dominant management theme in the decades to come. I shall therefore be enthusiastic in putting forward the theory that there is only one approach to explaining economic success: the degree of lived trust.

Only after making such an assessment shall I deal with the term "trust" itself. What is trust? What lies behind it? Is trust something irrational, something fundamentally good? Is it a moral concept, or, perhaps better, a term that has moral resonance for many people? This is where we enter a minefield of half-truths, misunderstandings and intellectual dead-ends. I will try to resolve these issues.

My second section is intended for those readers who are not just interested in trust in the everyday practical sense, but also keen to understand the power and limits of the concept. The practical people among you can safely skip it; I hope the theoreticians will excuse the brevity.

The third section is devoted to the practice of trust. How does the trust mechanism operate? What can you do as a manager to create trust? Which institutional conditions promote the development of trust? Which hinder it? In defiance to popular opinion, I will demonstrate that trust is not something to be built up slowly and indirectly as though it were an unintended by-product, but can be secured quickly and directly.

The title *Trust: The best way to manage* has a threefold message: trust is the first thing (and in a sense the only thing) that is truly decisive in a company; second, it is the basis of staff management; and third, it leads to values that are only revealed when it comes into operation.

You may have noticed that I have been treating trust as an *instrumental* value. I don't doubt that trust is valuable for its own sake. However, my concern is to remove trust from the romantic sphere and place it at the centre of a rational corporate policy that convinces as many people as possible. I advocate a trust that is calculable, that calculates, and that is worth while. A trust that is profitable – and by now the subject will be settled for some of you. A well-meaning person jumps up and says "Calculated trust? Engineering trust? How is that going to work? Trust doesn't thrive in the cold-store of economic profit maximization! How can you apprehend trust without making it disappear? And anyway, trust might sound cosy, but it's also naïve. It's nice to be a trustworthy person, but it's also very risky. As a philosophy of life, it leads to the morgue. You trust some people more, and some less. The reason why is not so important. Either trust is there or it isn't. What more is there to be said?"

That's as may be, but my intention here is to establish trust in a reasonable way. In particular, I want to deal with the *economic mechanism* behind the façade of trust. This is no easy task. The subject is full of paradoxes and ambiguities. There are no easy answers, no how-to checklists. Then again, if the subject hadn't been so elusive, I wouldn't have had to go to such trouble to investigate it. And beware: trust is a serious matter. The amused smile about the follies of internal company machinations seems to me to be out of place here. That's why I've resisted the temptation to engage in pointless provocation.

In the first part, my account makes some issues appear clearer and simpler than they really are on closer examination. The reasons for this are methodological: when I compare trust and mistrust, I am outlining the concept against a background that makes the contours recognizable. Taken to the extreme, any argument or stance becomes dangerous. This might apply especially to the subject of trust. The issue is one of degree. That's all I am concerned with.

When you read this book, many of you may find questions arising in your mind again and again: "Yes, but if ...." (I've had the same experience myself.) You may run scenarios through your mind and counter arguments with your own personal experiences. I can only ask you to bear with me, especially if you are a manager. After all, I have written this book primarily for you. In the end it is up to you whether you have the determination to tackle what is unfamiliar.

WHY TRUST?

An airport lounge in Vienna. I'm waiting for a return flight to Düsseldorf. Outside it's getting dark. That ineffable end-of-the-day atmosphere is seeping through the huge windows into the neon-lit room. A man is sitting opposite me. At about 7 p.m., he starts making telephone calls. The conversations all seem to go the same way. They are the usual calls checking the state of affairs. How are things going with that customer? What's happening with that project? Why has so-and-so not replied yet? What's happening tomorrow?

When he had gone through the whole list of calls, we started talking. I expressed my amazement that he was still making business calls so late. He said it was early, and he sometimes phoned people much later. He explained he made a point of having a brief chat with his staff every evening to see how his various projects were going. He wanted to be sure that everything was OK, especially with people who were working on difficult jobs.

At first I was impressed by his dedication to the job and loyalty to the company. Even after a long and hard day, he was still prepared to talk to his staff. And apparently they were also prepared to talk to their boss at 7 p.m. Amazing! But then doubts crept in. Could it be that he only made these telephone calls because he didn't trust his staff? Could it be that he brought his mistrust into their living rooms because he didn't trust *them* to ring *him* if they needed to talk to someone?

Because it is missing: An assessment

A CEO whose company publicly has identified trust as one of its five key values addresses the person leading the discussion in a determined way and says "It is a matter of urgent necessity that we do more to address the subject of trust. It is lacking everywhere." There are nods of agreement among the other members of the board. The presenter waits a moment. Then he asks "And you? Do you trust each other?"

At the 55th Annual Conference of German Business Managers (Deutscher Betriebswirtschaftertag) in September 2001 in Berlin, people agreed: in the long run it is intangibles that increase corporate value. These intangibles include knowledge, talent, brand and (relevant to all three) trust. It was said that trust has never been as valuable as it is today.

Trust is now a very high priority. Financial markets demand it because trust in management is reflected in a company's share price. Newspapers tell us that trust is the only thing that can help build confidence in economic development. A journalist questions whether we can trust politicians. Opinion researchers want to know which politicians inspire the most confidence.

Trust is invoked, desired and demanded everywhere. Why?

Because it is lacking. People talk about trust when it is missing. It is conspicuous by its absence. People aren't exaggerating when they say that the more talk there is about trust, the worse the situation. When the subject of trust breaks the surface, it's an unmistakable sign of crisis.

Something is not quite right when a board of directors appeals for trust from the staff: "...and that is why I am asking for your trust, especially in these difficult times." Or a bank uses the advertising slogan "Trust is the key to everything." There is something dubious about discussing trust. It can evidently only be experienced as something lost or broken. That's why it is easier to explain why we mistrust someone than to say why we trust them.

In companies, trust is ostensibly the most important factor in co-operation. Yet it is frequently the rarest thing too. When asked about their management qualities, managers like to reply "I trust my staff." At the same time, they wish they enjoyed more trust from their superiors. One level further up the hierarchy, the story is the same: people believe in their own ability to trust, but complain about a lack of trust from higher up. What's going on? Is this merely a difference of perception?

The answer starts to emerge when one asks managers about their weak points. They often mention their perfectionism. They smile and admit they tend to intervene and declare issues to be matters for management. The idea is deeply internalized: "You always have to keep an eye on them!" These managers keep a constant eye on their staff and keep asking "Are they going to fulfil their role? Are they up to the job? Do they have enough experience to do what needs to be done?" One step lower down the hierarchy, such an attitude is interpreted as mistrust. The desire for more trust is born.

It is true that the division of tasks between staff in a company is inconceivable without a certain degree of trust in the continuity of other people's actions and in their predictability, honesty and willingness to co-operate. To delegate, a manager has to trust a member of staff to carry out a task. But trust in a subordinate's competence seems not to extend beyond the manager's current field of monitoring. This is demonstrated by the obsession with controlling external workers. Information technology has made it possible to introduce new control mechanisms that operate over long distances, even where it has quickly become apparent that they don't really allow effective control. We now have all the technical means to work in a relaxed way wherever we are. Flexible, connected, supported, integrating all areas of competence – even if someone has a cold or is heavily pregnant. And remote management meets with resistance in most companies, with their old-fashioned work organization cloaked in a modern disguise: duty to attend, control systems, meeting rituals. Remote management becomes a cynical means of hidden control (H. Rust). The key problem is mistrust.

Even though people may seem proactive and decisive during discussions in the company corridors, they also seem inhibited and hesitant. The views they express, with their "synergies" and "learning organizations," sound like exam answers that have been learnt by heart. It isn't difficult to identify entire departments of mistrust that spend their time checking and monitoring people to see whether they are doing what they are supposed to be doing. Their managers are skilled in creating false alarms and putting their victims under constant nervous stress with forms and regulations. Staff, it would seem, are a hostile species who should be suspected, investigated and reduced to the lowest common denominator, for all their diversity.

Mistrust dominates both sides of the relationship: managers' with staff, and staff's with managers. Management doesn't trust staff to make decisions in the company's best interests. Staff greet management's actions with cynicism because they don't believe management is competent to take responsibility for long-term workable solutions to problems. They suspect that managers won't keep to agreements, that they are less interested in the company's interests than their own and that they are generally untrustworthy. For their part, managers suspect that staff dislike working and need to be pushed before they will work at all. Underneath all this lies a fundamental belief that you can't trust unfettered human nature. There is also *horizontal* mistrust, which is understandable under competitive conditions. Colleagues become opponents, and anything that depends on staff co-operating with each other doesn't happen.

Ornaments of mistrust include: anonymity in inquiries; secretiveness about salaries; the flood of endorsements and memorandums ("Can you put that in writing for me?"); the institutionalized practice of returning delegated tasks to the person who delegates them; the narrow-minded obsession with measuring ("You can't manage what you can't measure"); and the boss who always says "Remember to copy me in on your e-mails." And there are many more: the security measures people take before they make decisions; the habit of always playing it safe; the meetings that get bigger and bigger; the mounting productivity checks; the attendance time clock (now a time-monitoring computer program that cries out "I don't trust you!" to a member of staff in the morning, but is disdainfully ignored by the heads of department); the pressure toward total control of communication.

Managers tell their staff they are only allowed to speak positively about the company in the outside world. They draw up function charts that specify in minute detail who can say what outside the company. They compel their staff always to use the same words at the beginning of a telephone conversation; they specify that the same content must always be presented in the same way. And then there is the secretary who despite repeated requests is refused permission to use a master key for the coffee machine. Instead of being able to fill whole jugs using the key, she has to press the button 120 times for 120 cups. In this age of genetic engineering, we won't have long to wait before we see people having control chips implanted in them.

These manifestations can become quite bizarre. A journalist called Eike Gebhardt told me he spent €2,000 on a flight from Stuttgart to Cairo via Düsseldorf, but it took four months for his radio station to reimburse him because it insisted on checking whether he was allowed to claim the customary €7 daily allowance for foreign assignments for this particular flight.

Mistrust sometimes appears as early as job interviews. Many interviewers adopt the approach of trying to get a lot out of the applicant in the shortest possible time. This sends the message "You are not important" to the applicant, and rests on the assumption that he is hiding something and trying to present himself as better than he actually is. Some people watch each other covertly and see deceitfulness in every utterance; they think others are trying to fool them, and look for something incongruous behind what is being claimed. The interviewee is suspected of embellishing his abilities; the interviewer is suspected of embellishing the company. Employment interviews are often a breeding ground for mistrust.

For many people, though, mistrust is at its height in the way working time is handled. There has been much debate in Germany about trust-based working time. The expression speaks volumes: it highlights the exceptional nature of the aspect of trust. Is there such a thing as "mistrust-based working time"? In 1972, Hewlett-Packard gave up recording employees' working hours; its CEO, Lewis Platt, said that this step was based on faith in its staff. I don't doubt Platt's motive, but isn't this a calculated cost? Everyone knows that time-recording systems are vulnerable to manipulation. Moreover, we need to ask ourselves whether a purely quantitative, time-based concept of work is realistic nowadays. Shouldn't our thinking be geared more to output than input?

Quite a lot of companies have now tried to introduce trust-based working time. However, it frequently fails because of mutual mistrust. Those at the top worry that costs might rise if time is no longer monitored, and complain "It's always the same ones who work, and the same ones who take it easy." Those at the bottom are afraid they will be treated unfairly and exploited at busy times if they can't present the boss with their printed attendance certificate. Nothing gives. Mistrust is the poison that paralyses everything.

One board of directors has to give consent for a divisional manager to help out. Key service staff are monitored by video camera in order to reduce losses of metal parts. Audit-mania rules, with an excessive need for independent checking. A new director with a fresh attitude comes in, and is keen on dialogue – too much dialogue for some HR managers. They send a strictly confidential e-mail: "The HR managers for Europe have decided that all communication with the new director must take place via us. There is to be no direct contact."

Many managers are obsessed with the idea that their staff want to deceive them. They install one system after another to prevent people getting away. Daily control procedures multiply. There are waves of reports with no measure or limit. You have to post your projects on the intranet on Monday so that central management has an overview. At the same time, small jobs that people used to deal with on the side are given the status of real projects. After the former IBM manager Dan Cerutti become a software entrepreneur, he said that in his old job he had been dealing with managers who assumed that no member of staff ever wanted to work. This mistrust was expressed in everything they did.

That's the way it seems to be: a lot of companies are organizations of suspicion. Managers produce huge manuals out of mistrust, pinning down even the smallest role in the company. They don't believe that people want to do good work. A deep-seated insecurity, covered by a mask of rationality, makes managers into policemen patrolling a precinct. They have no trust in their staff's self-imposed quality standards, and are reluctant to allow them to find their own ways of achieving objectives.

The ingrained habit of mistrust is clear from the things people say: "Everyone distrusts everyone in the factory." "You can't trust anyone an inch here." "Every movement is monitored." "Honesty is naïvety here." "It's dangerous to express an opinion." The CSM – career-shortening move – is soon reached. A foreign CEO isn't trusted ("He doesn't even speak our language and he'll probably be off again soon").

Credibility is lacking everywhere you look. The company's information policy is met with great scepticism, as are financial projections, HR policy and plans for restructuring: "People aren't putting their cards on the table." "The company magazine is pure propaganda." There is a yawning gap between speech and action: "I'm disappointed by management's decisions, which are being reversed just six months later." "The policy here seems to be 'who cares what I said yesterday.'" "Today it'll be like this, and tomorrow it'll be like that." And trust doesn't exactly increase when people notice the discrepancy between petty economizing measures and authorization policies on the one hand and the enormous amounts paid to top management on the other.

Many people have had enough of the increase in regulations and mechanisms for checking and justifying actions. They see all this red tape as a hindrance to their actual work: "Too much bureaucracy," "Mounting floods of paperwork," "Filling in forms for everything," "More and more administrative work that adds absolutely no value." "Working by predetermined procedures regardless of whether it makes sense or not." "You notice straight away that something isn't right." Occasions for mistrust occur constantly. People are being deceitful almost the whole time, as nearly every official communication seems to suggest.

A study of the state of the chemical industry (Kiefer et al. 2001) found an acute lack of trust: "Not one of the replies gave any indication of a trusting relationship with senior management." Indeed, staff seemed incredibly alienated from them: "What is the management up to?" "I don't believe they care about the company's interests. They are pursuing their careers at the expense of the company." The study established that not all negative feelings make people tend to withdraw. In terms of consequences for the company; mistrust must be clearly distinguished from other negative feelings such as anger, worry and disappointment. Everyday irritations are blamed on the company, but don't affect people's performance of their personal tasks. Mistrust, on the other hand, leads to inner withdrawal both from the company *and* from the employee's own work. Someone who lacks trust is less prepared to engage himself in the company and the job and to remain in the company and the job.

There are many sayings in circulation that rationalize the obsession with monitoring and control: trust is good but control is better; trust must be earned; opportunities create thieves. The more serious, intellectual managers often develop brilliant rhetoric to justify mistrust. Disconcerting stories are frequently told about breaches of trust, deception and malicious conduct. The grave consequences of a breach of trust are illustrated in numerous examples: the billions lost by Barings Bank in 1995 thanks to the broker Nicholas Leeson; the damage done to the Sumitomo Bank in 1996 by Yasuo Hamanaka, the head of copper trading. In 1999, Electrolux Deutschland incurred a loss of DM55 million because of unauthorized forward exchange transactions carried out by a member of staff. The names

Schneider, Flowtex, Swissair, ABB and Enron stand for incompetence, greed and in some cases criminal acts. The new global markets are turning out to be a cautionary tale of adventurous valuation and accounting methods whose main purpose is to pull the wool over investors' eyes.

But the pendulum has swung too far. Companies have paid too much attention to risk limitation. The situation has been turned upside down. Normally, reasons are required for mistrust but not for trust. People don't ask "Why do you trust me?" In companies it is the other way around: mistrust doesn't need any reason, but trust does. This is especially true when something has gone wrong – and of course something will always go wrong. Many companies have gone a long way toward the regulation end of the spectrum. Then the security fanatics come to power. Mistrust becomes the norm. When that happens, trust becomes a sin.

Let's take a look at the structural background. The economy doesn't seem to be concerned with trust. Economic behaviour (profit maximization, developing competitive strategies, exploiting information) seems to positively exclude it. A survey of literature on business management shows that economic intelligence is geared to the second-hand car model – the model of maximum mistrust.

We have reached the limits of this paradigm. The prolongation capability (a concept from biological evolution) is used up. No further growth is possible within the current mode of thought. Economic success is already fragile. A small change in environmental conditions frequently brings about a drastic decline in prolongation capacity. Many companies are held in an invisible prison. Red tape, rigid administration procedures and mushrooming regulations prevent any emergence of business dynamism. The walls and bars of this prison are the basic assumptions about the economy and human behaviour.

It is becoming ever clearer that the big old instruments of control – power and money – are no longer adequate to co-ordinate human activity in companies, especially in an information society and in fast-operating markets. More and more situations arise that can't be managed. We're talking about things that can't be forced. Success with intangible assets can no longer be achieved where there is too much control. Anything that depends on the willingness of staff to co-operate with each other can't be controlled directly. Control ceases to work; trust has to supplement the old means of management, and increasingly to replace them. Trust is becoming the key factor in successful company management.

If you have followed me so far in this analysis, you will have seen there is a gross disparity between what's needed and what exists: how much trust is there already and how much more is needed. There are some traditional reasons for trust and some very modern ones. Let's take a closer look at them.

Because it allows flexible organization

According to Francis Fukuyama, the welfare and competitiveness of a nation are determined by a single pervasive cultural characteristic: the degree of trust in the society. Some economists even consider the level of trust to be more important than natural resources to the prosperity of national economies. Twenty-five years ago, the American Nobel Laureate Kenneth Arrow wrote "Virtually every commercial transaction has within itself an element of trust, certainly any transaction conducted over a period of time. It can be plausibly argued that much of the economic backwardness in the world can be explained by the lack of mutual confidence." The cohesive effect of trust is conveyed in numerous metaphors: trust is the cement, the band, the oil that keeps the wheels of an organization running (W. Bennis / B. Nanus). In fact, really productive co-operation is inconceivable without trust. Trust brings hidden energy resources for co-operation to the surface.

This has been known for a long time. But what if the global is almost more familiar than the domestic? If the longing for familiar conditions is now wanderlust? What if the nature of the economy is becoming global (de-localized) and trading is taking place in intangible services? And, in the extreme case, what if the virtual company integrates cross-company production links, intensive co-operation agreements and cross-company division of labour without itself having a specific location or duration?

Trust is increasingly becoming a condition for organizations' very existence. This is because "the value of an organization is no longer measured by the balance that it tries to bring about between its individual parts or the clarity of its parameters but by the number of openings and interfaces that it can organize with everything external" (Jean-Marie Guehenno). We are entering the age of zero knowledge management and open systems: strategic alliances, outsourcing, agency contracts, new public management, internationalization, franchising, working from home, mobile working and network organizations that use communication technology to operate without physical mobility. All these break down existing organizational parameters.

The management of organizations has extended beyond national frontiers and continents for a long time now. Working groups that were once locally based have transformed themselves into virtual teams: staff, departments and whole divisions of companies work in conjunction with each other but at different locations within the country, in different countries or even on different continents. Companies aren't national organizations operating in enclosed spaces. The factory gate is no longer a reliable indicator of identity. Suppliers build their own branch establishments at the factory premises and make decisions on site with the customer. At many offices, the cleaning staff now spend more time working there than the people for whom the office was built. The idea that staff work within the company while customers and suppliers operate outside need no longer apply. Dirk Baecker pointed out that corporate groups are shrinking and becoming clubhouses that people visit on account of their excellent cuisine.

Trust plays a prominent role, in fact the decisive role, in international co-operation between companies. Irrespective of which form of co-operation they choose (licensing, franchising, contract manufacturing), management is trust management. We can see the extent to which trust has become a hard factor if we look at the example of mergers and acquisitions: a large number of failed mergers are attributed to the fact that trust has either not developed or has been destroyed. The systematic withholding of information in the negotiating phase creates a great deal of mistrust, not only with staff but also with customers: for example, Rolls-Royce suffered a considerable drop in sales after being taken over by VW. Customers weren't informed about "their" manufacturer's future for a long time, and they feared a loss of quality and prestige. Even suppliers tend to be proactive when mergers take place; in other words, they raise their prices. And then people are confronted with the reality of "Today a competitor, tomorrow a partner." I hear people say "I've been doing battle for years with these people who've been playing rotten tricks on me with customers, and now I'm supposed to trust them?"

Take the example of DaimlerChrysler: the Americans came

27

unprepared and wanted to talk without an agenda. The Germans were armed to the teeth, and wanted detailed agendas. The Germans produced minutes for every meeting; the Americans confined themselves to memos.

As actual presence becomes less necessary and our world becomes more virtual, trust becomes more important as an organizational principle. We use the internet to communicate with people we have never seen and probably never will see. And the more companies open up and working conditions become less concrete, the less well people know each other. So in the modern world, trust in our partners can no longer be based on familiarity, experience and consistency. The sheer size of companies makes it almost impossible to observe behaviour over a particular period from close up so as to build up personal trust. This is the big new reality:

It is no longer possible for trust to develop out of familiarity.

Trust facilitates co-ordinated action between partners who are and remain unknown to each other. It is a substitute for knowledge about the other party and his motives. If ambitious commercial goals are to be achieved, we have to trust people we don't know personally. Many find this difficult. The barriers include a lack of ability to trust, an antiquated trust that derives its stability from the predictability of circumstances, and a corporate reality that wants clear structures and fixed classifications: managers who know the people they trust and trust those they know.

We are faced with a situation without historical precedents: the need for trust is growing rapidly, while the traditional sources are drying up. And the larger the company, the greater the need for trust and the more difficult it is to fulfil it. Consequently, we are experiencing an upward revaluation of trust as an organizational principle.

Because it facilitates reorganization

Companies have to be flexible in today's markets. They need to be capable of constant adaptation and change. Trust is an indispensable element in the transformation process that leads away from rigid hierarchies toward flexible, customer-oriented corporate structures. Empowerment, business process optimization, flat hierarchies, teamwork, the learning organization – none of these essential business initiatives can succeed without a sound foundation of trust. Companies are transformed when people trust.

People know that companies have to change to survive. They aren't blind to the fact that profitability and welfare are often in conflict. They see that there is no such thing as true job security. They also know that it can be better for everyone if managers are separated from divisions in companies. So why do we so often see resistance? When people sense that restructuring is always to their disadvantage. When they are the sole losers. When they believe that companies no longer care about staff.

We could put it another way: staff support changes when plans for reorganization are not primarily to their detriment. They need to be able to trust management in this respect. If people are to commit to more than mere adaptation or maximizing of their own interests, they need a feeling of belonging, the certainty that management is favourably disposed toward them, that it cares about them, that it isn't guided exclusively by the requirements of the financial markets. Of course, this applies only to issues that can be resolved by balancing the needs of different parties in the business context. Staff trust when managers, as the agents of capital, don't as a matter of principle move the lines of conflict between the different interests to their disadvantage. A businessman friend of mine put it like this "Your employees don't care how much you know until they know how much you care."

This trust relationship has, however, been put to a hard test. Ongoing changes and initiatives erode the reliability, routines and institutions that give rise to trust. People are no longer sure whether decades of commitment will be rewarded by their company. "Change!" is often an appeal not to imagination but to one's ability to cope. One of the greatest mistakes in company management is to assume that trust will reappear by itself after traumatic events that affect jobs (redundancy, restructuring, mergers). That's simply unrealistic.

However, to address the problem properly, we need to look at the other side: there are old, hardened ways of looking at things that inhibit trust on the staff side too. The classic division into two camps (capitalist companies and management on one side and exploited employees on the other) is reflected in the divergence between management and shop stewards' committee. It is unfortunate if staff take the view that only shop stewards from their own ranks can legitimately represent their interests. And as this view is the basis for a shop stewards' committee, it will be reflected by the committee on an ongoing basis. There is no room for the idea that representation of interests is actually the task of management. There isn't much room for trust in the classical model: that lot up there and these ones down here.

Because it produces loyal customers

Wherever you look, trust sells. Take the grocery trade: we know that convenience is the most important reason for preferring one supplier to another. However, if people are to turn into regular customers, the company concerned must pay attention to the trustworthiness factor. Trust requires care, attention, even challenge. The very first time people experience disappointment, they start looking for another supplier. And as disappointments are not exactly a rare event, trust falters and the number of partners increases. Consequently, many manufacturers woo trust with money-back guarantees or extended rights of return. The word "trust" is prominently displayed on every other trading item in America. The retro wave within the car and clothing industry is a reaction to the growing need for trust. When products appear with names like Granny's Apple Sauce, the consumer imagines a grandmother picking the apples with her own hands and cooking them with a lot of love and no artificial additives. Car manufacturers embark on highly publicized recall campaigns in order to demonstrate their heartfelt concern about their customers' safety. Delta Lloyd Investment offers a fund with a portfolio that people can check. Updates are shown daily on the internet after the market closes. "Transparency creates trust," says CEO Holger Dersch; he believes that he gains a competitive advantage in this way. The seminar market is full of offers that are popular only because customer trust has become top priority.

The sociologist Niklas Luhmann has talked about the law of meeting again in relation to trust. It is more difficult to commit a breach of trust if people know they are likely to meet again and have to look each other in the eye. Looking at it the other way around, a breach of trust is easier to commit if people can presume it won't be discovered and they won't meet the other person again. In the age of information technology, the law of meeting again is becoming topical. It is true that customer relationships are becoming more sophisticated and there is less personal contact. However, customers and suppliers encounter each other on the internet; customers exchange views; and it is difficult for abuses of trust to remain undiscovered.

People are using the internet more and more, and if they encounter a company with a supposedly first-class service that doesn't even reply to e-mails, they tell other people about it. Several cases have come to light in which angry customers have used their own websites to inform the public about poor treatment by companies (usually trading groups). Some have been forced to undertake major restructuring of their operations.

Customer trust is above all trust in prices. Ikea guarantees its customers unmatched cost-effectiveness that they don't even have to compare with competitors. It was customer trust that made it possible for Aldi to sell €200 million-worth of unbranded computers in two days. In the United States, Wal-Mart doesn't have the cheapest offer anywhere, but it has succeeded in convincing customers that the price is the best it can do for the product and that if other companies offer it cheaper, there are other reasons such as trying to lure new customers with cut prices. It is no accident that the biography of the founder, Sam Walton, has the title *In Sam We Trust*. Bob Carpenter, head of Dollar General, said: "It took us a long time to achieve high quality at favorable prices in the market. We will not do anything that could damage customers' trust in our prices."

In times when products are becoming increasingly similar, intangible motives are playing a growing role in purchasing decisions. We might even say: *companies don't sell products, they sell trust.* That's why brands are so important: a brand is a crystal-lization of trust. The advertising industry talks about trust marks, which reduce complexity and function as a navigation aid. They make it easier for customers to decide whether or not a product deserves trust, and save time by sparing customers the need to obtain information in complex markets and compare all the products on offer. This is becoming all the more important as people are pressed for time. Virgin Group boss Sir Richard Branson has understood this. He has managed to make Virgin a symbol for "small, human, active." "All power to the people" is Virgin's idea. If Virgin enters the telecommunications market (not part of its traditional core business), everyone knows immediately what that means: low costs for customers.

Customer loyalty has always been interpreted as an expression of customers' trust in a company. However, if we define companies as expert systems, then the reintroduction of social relationships in local contexts is through people located at their access points, i.e. staff. Every member of staff can build a trust bridge that ties customers to the company. From the customer's point of view, the member of staff is not working for the company; he *is* the company.

What Hans Domizlaff wrote in 1929 is still true today: "The value of a brand is based on the consumer's familiarity with the 'face' of the branded article. A branded article is the product of a personality and its most effective backing is through the stamp of a personality." Staff embody trust, as it were: experts and expertise coincide. And it pays: the longer a customer relationship lasts, the more profitable it is, because customers become less and less price-sensitive. And then the customer tells you "You may be a little bit too expensive, but if we trust each other, it's not a problem."

The more important is customer trust in what the company

provides, the greater the importance of the organization's decentralized pre-production processes (rather than its headquarters).

I myself developed trust in a make of car that I have stuck with for years because of a salesman at a local dealer. He was fair, he wasn't pushy, and he advised me in a personal way. He even pointed out a few of the product's weak points. The first time I brought the car to the workshop for a service, I started to get to know the other members of staff. I'm now convinced of the company's integrity. My trust in the salesman has extended to the whole organization. Obviously, this can work the other way around too: mistrust in respect of one person can extend to the entire company.

Because it makes companies fast

Martin Sanders has finally found his dream home after years of searching. But other potential buyers are also interested. The location is popular, and the price is OK. The vendors, an elderly couple, have a "first come, first served" attitude. Speed is of the essence. So Martin rushes to his savings bank, where he has been a customer since childhood, fills in a mortgage application, supplies details of assets, liabilities and recent financial statements, attaches information about the property he wishes to purchase, indicates the urgency of the situation – and then waits. A few days go by and he doesn't hear anything. When he enquires, he is told that the matter is being processed. Then he waits a few more days.

Martin Sanders becomes impatient. He rings again. Now he is told that someone at head office has stipulated that he must submit further documents. He is annoyed; why didn't they phone him? He obtains the documents as quickly as possible, delivers them by hand, and waits again. Time is running out, and his dream house is disappearing; he phones the branch again. The person he speaks to says they can't deal with it, head office has to do so. "Hold on a moment, I'll put you through." The woman at the other end isn't aware of the loan application, but after a bit of searching she finds it. "The member of staff responsible is on holiday for a few days but he left a note saying that we still need the following documents..." Martin is also required to produce his divorce certificate! Divorce certificate? It's the last straw.

The same day, Martin Sanders goes to the bank around the corner. He has to submit a lot of documents all over again, but he senses that they are making a real effort to give him a decision within 48 hours. He gets his loan. He gets his dream house. He is no longer a savings bank customer.

The market punishes people who are late. Of course, all financial institutions are bound by legislation relating to their procedures; they have to ask applicants to disclose their financial circumstances. However, how people deal with the law and handle matters internally depends on the trust situation in the company. Many people who obstruct business at head office have never seen a customer; they work through their lists and make decisions on paper. They don't trust the customer or their own staff on site, who have known some customers for decades.

Today's intense international competition knows only three dimensions: speed, speed and speed. Economy of speed is the commercial factor of the century. Speed is becoming more and more important for innovation, production times, logistical processes and submission of tenders. Markets don't allow us to spend ages going through hierarchical levels to obtain a decision. Customers are no longer willing to wait for a company to work out all its internal checks and balances and overcome its trust problems. They will go elsewhere. The problem is addressed in the subject of time to market: time has to be invested where it is needed – with the customer.

However, prevailing management practice hasn't kept pace with the environment. It has hardly changed since 1950. It is risk-averse. The thick bundles of contracts assembled by a legal department several people strong come from a time when gaps in the market were like the valleys between mountains; nowadays they are mere crevasses.

If we take the past as a yardstick, then only a third of the companies that exist now will survive the next 20 years. The others will go under or be sold because they are too slow to react to market changes. This is why the greatest management challenge for the foreseeable future is simply to become much quicker. Companies must organize themselves in such a way that they change as quickly as economic conditions do. In an information economy, it isn't the working time invested that matters, but the speed with which problems are identified and solved. To increase it, we have to change the system, which is built on power, internal competition and adaptation. If you want to make your company faster, you can do it only through trust. Only then can you react quickly to what customers want. A person acts faster and more decisively if he is not preoccupied with the possibility that he might be breaking some strict rule. He will work faster if he doesn't need to get three sets of approval for every step he takes, and if he doesn't have to read through his target agreement, job description or ISO manual. Sport has the expression "fast break" where the whole pitch is surveyed in a few moves; without trust in the players, it is impossible.

We all feel the challenges of global competition and the erosion of certain knowledge and agreed codes. We know that if we aren't dynamic in the way we co-operate, the pressure of the market with its requirement for ever-greater speed will throw us out of the competition. We scan the horizon for technical and organizational solutions. We never notice that the greatest resource is right there in front of us: the human capacity for trust.

It is both astonishing and sad that trust is least evident when a company is deep in crisis. In such situations, much money is invested in bringing in outside consultants; they may have the benefit of objectivity, but they never have the necessary experience or real inside knowledge. Instead of using their own staff's problem-solving ability, companies engage consultants to solve fundamental problems and develop new strategies.

Despite good intentions, a lot of companies have difficulty moving beyond old rules. At Bosch, a company that has represented Germany Inc. for some time (authoritarian, punctual, old-fashioned), the head, Hermann Scholl, is in favour of reform: "We have seen that we are not moving forward fast enough." Teams have been set up to drive the time-to-market process. A BeQIK ("be quick") initiative was launched, and staff were groomed for speed. However, the Swabian cultural to revolution isn't making great progress because the root of the problem isn't being tackled. Until senior management cuts down the thicket of controls, regulations and justification rituals, the organization will be simply too cumbersome for an age of global sourcing and fast-integrating markets. On 25 September 2001, the *Frankfurter Allgemeine Zeitung* reported that Blaupunkt, a Bosch subsidiary, had lost an order for navigation systems from DaimlerChrysler worth over €400 million to competitors (Siemens VDO Automotive and Becker). It hadn't been able to process the order quickly enough.

Trust may seem an extraordinary attribute to mention in the context of organizational procedures. However, it will be anything but irrelevant for someone who has been dealing with turnaround processes, where only one thing counts: speed. Normally, after the downsizing phase, the turnaround manager quickly selects a group of people to whom he gives one thing above all: trust. He discusses with them the key information needed for the company's survival, and they're off. He can't afford to construct elaborate control systems, checks and reporting procedures. It takes too long, and before you know it, the patient is dead.

The fact that trust works, and quickly, is demonstrated by a banking system that has been in operation for centuries. The Chinese call it *Fei Chien* (flying money); from India to the Arabic world and East Africa it is known as *Hawala*. In the Afghan language Pashto, the Pakistani language Urdu and the Indian language Hindi, *Hawala* simply means trust. Every year approximately $300 billion is transferred by this system. Money is sent around the world via private trustees on the basis of a handshake. The money is paid in at a shop somewhere (Berlin, say) with a codeword. The customer or a trusted person can have the amount paid out in Islamabad by a partner in the system provided the codeword is given. A phone call is sufficient. Hawala is based on something older than the banking system: trust. Flying money: all our ideas about free movement (flying, gliding, floating) are connected in one way or another with trust.

To avoid any misunderstanding: we don't get things done faster by rushing around and doing many things at once. We need to learn that speeding up has nothing to do with running faster, working harder or working longer. The way to get faster is to create working conditions in which trust grows. Trust is speed.

At Southwest Airlines, people tell a story about Gary Baron, executive vice-president, who is currently reorganizing the company's $700 million cleaning service. It seems he met his CEO,

Herb Kelleher, in the corridor. He handed his boss a three-page summary of his organizational plan. Kelleher read it and said: "OK, get going!" The matter was decided in less than four minutes. Two people trusted each other.

Because it supports knowledge transfer and entrepreneurialism

Knowledge is the resource of the future. A company's shared knowledge and the associated innovative ability of its staff are competitive advantages with a high degree of protection, being difficult to copy. But staff are seldom prepared to share their knowledge. Why? They would then be dispensable, endangering their jobs and relinquishing power. Knowledge management is, in the words of Lutz von Rosenstiel, "expropriation by experts." That's why it fails in cultures of mistrust.

People will share their ideas only if they can do so without incurring any disadvantages. The more people trust each other, the more they will share knowledge without the need to make rules, negotiate contracts or engage lawyers. In companies with a low level of trust, people will guard their ideas; at most they will share ideas at a formal, superficial level, and only then if asked expressly. That's why employee suggestion systems are characteristic of mistrust cultures: they work on the assumption that people won't attempt to improve working processes of their own accord. They assume that managers and staff don't talk to each other. They emphasize hierarchy, bureaucracy and the view that thinking is an exceptional event for the underlings.

When we look at the subject of knowledge and entrepreneurialism, we can see that the classic management mechanisms (namely power and money) are ineffective as a means of co-ordinating human actions. The decisive factor is almost exclusively the "horizontal" trust of staff among themselves and the "vertical" trust between management and staff. Without horizontal trust, there can be no transfer of knowledge; without vertical trust, no willingness to take risks.

Because it facilitates creativity and innovation

R. Glanville describes the experience of a head teacher who wanted to do something nice for his staff at Christmas. He decided on a small present. However, he was new in his post and didn't know the staff as individuals, so it seemed impossible to find 60 personal gifts. Instead, he bought 60 presents, put them in Christmas wrapping paper and piled them in a heap. During the Christmas celebration, everyone took a present from the heap. Out of the 60 people, only two picked presents that they didn't like, but they were able to exchange them.

What does this have to do with innovation, creativity and trust? This way of giving presents changed the attitude of the staff from "Will I get what I want?" to "What surprise is waiting for me?" It opened their minds to something unexpected. The result was uncertain, as it always is with creative processes. The giver had decided to relinquish control of the outcome and trust the process.

For many companies, innovation is synonymous with survival. Innovation is capable of defining new markets in a matter of weeks. When the innovation engine falters, companies fall behind and sooner or later have to leave the race.

If we agree with Francis Bacon, who believes creative curiosity is simply part of human nature, companies should have no problem. But consider the reality: management homes in on two things, creativity and innovation, which they hold up as totems while simultaneously doing everything to hinder their staff's enthusiasm for discovery and invention. In response to the questions "Where can innovation thrive? In what creative climate? In what atmosphere?," people will come up with many locations, but usually exclude just one: their own company. Quite a few conditions there are simply anti-innovative. Most companies are short of intellectual risk capital; ideas about security take priority. Innovation is good, as long as it stops at our own office door. Everyone wants reform provided it starts with somebody else.

Trust along the vertical axis is especially necessary. We decide to trust someone after we have calculated the probable loss if we are disappointed, and the likely gain if things turn out as we hope. Creative work is fragile and uncertain: ideas have to be developed, proposed, tested and justified or abandoned. People engage in such a process only when they feel secure, in an atmosphere of trust, respect and good will. Trust makes it easier to cope with deviations from routines and rules, especially when innovations and experiments end in error or failure. That's why entrepreneurialism arises only in companies with high tolerance of errors, where people know that failure isn't going to be remorselessly punished. Creative people, people who take things on, are risk-takers. They must be supported with trust. Entrepreneurialism and trust are inseparable.

Anyone who thinks seriously about it knows that creativity comes at a cost. When new things emerge and old things are abandoned, we sacrifice the trusted for the untrusted. The mutiplicity of thoughts that bring about innovation can be irritating and impair efficiency, but they bear rich fruit. If you want to get the innovation engine going, you have to gear your organization to flexibility, not efficiency. Creativity thrives under a condition that is foreign to the very nature of organization: dispensing with justification. Trust, in other words.

Anyone seeking creativity has to reduce the pressure for justification. Accept uncertainty. Let go. Surrender control. That's because the new can seldom be justified from the point of view of what already exists. Indeed, new things that are successfully justified are often old things in disguise that prevail without being recognized for what they are. Many aspects of creativity can't be justified immediately or in absolute terms. Creativity would be strangled at birth by the demand for justification. Trust means having courage, being daring. I don't know who said it, but I'm not ashamed to repeat it: "Everything that's really new in the world comes from those who dare to be a bit crazy."

The enemies of creativity are mistrust and justification. If you put people under constant pressure to justify what they do, if you don't trust, if you don't take risks, you can't expect creativity to develop. To demand "Be creative!" is paradoxical. No one can do that to order. You have to allow the non-rational, even the irrational, to be expressed if you want new things to come into the world. This in itself is paradoxical, because bringing about unpredictable events from which fruitful developments can flow is not irrational, but rational when these developments lead to solutions that work better on all levels than the previous solutions did. What's needed is a territory free from justification and standardization – a territory in which people can move wherever their intuition takes them instead of feeling constantly under scrutiny. Isn't it fitting to encourage the non-rational in situations where no great damage is to be feared and where something new can be expected to develop? It comes close to play – another thing that people can do only in an atmosphere of trust.

Because it saves costs

Shiv Nadar, CEO at HCL, says: "Bureaucracy is always a sign of lack of trust and mutual respect and regard in a company. Constantly looking over someone else's shoulder doesn't work. It merely introduces a cost factor, which does not generate any value." We could even say that regulation destroys value. Controlling activities sap people's creative energies and motivation: "I've had enough of justification mania; this is a command economy." "I'm surrounded by fast-developing but shoddy computer systems for registering things, recording time, measuring performance, checking and planning." "Nowadays you need authorization for anything and everything. The financial control is so petty that I have to go through official channels for every little thing." "I'm constantly asked to be innovative, but at the same time any possibility of responsibility and initiative is taken away."

These costs can't even be measured; they are incalculable. The same goes for the missed opportunities for co-operation, which aren't calculated simply because they can't be quantified and don't appear anywhere. Here is my theory: if the purpose of a company is to develop and sell goods and services, then half its activities are pointless. We could put it like this: half the pool of costs in most companies is caused by mistrust. Administrative costs that are growing faster than turnover can be a warning sign of this kind of unproductive development.

Mistrust pushes up costs. The routines of daily co-operation can only develop in a cost-effective way against a background of trust. We can save the resources we have to keep in reserve to cover nasty surprises, so cutting out a whole layer of costs:
The costs of frequent selection and deselection of contractual parties. A high fluctuation rate incurs particularly high costs in the

case of knowledge-intensive goods, because they are difficult to test in advance. You can't test lawyers before you engage them, and if you don't trust your lawyer, it will cost you. You carry out selection interviews and obtain extra opinions, which all costs time and money. If you want to get a second opinion to be on the safe side as a customer, a person seeking advice or a patient, the costs of obtaining the additional information need to be taken into account.

The costs of frictional losses caused by permanent agreements, negotiations and renegotiations. Every negotiation, every draft contract and every agreement increases transaction costs. Useful as they may be in individual cases, their benefits need to be weighed against their costs. And anyone who operates in today's turbulent markets will be able to adhere to agreements on targets only by paying the price of constant renegotiation. Often, targets aren't worth the paper they are written on just 14 days after an agreement. Many managers complain that trying to be fair leaves them drowning in a mass of renegotiation. Yet the purpose of forming an agreement in the first place was to reduce transaction costs.

The costs of explicit contractual security measures and monitoring activities. The costs of controlling specialists, especially those who work with their intellect, are prohibitively steep. Visual control (is he doing what he is supposed to do?), management by walking about, centralized control procedures, advanced work-checking technologies – all these things are highly expensive. Many sociological studies have shown that the costs of a monitoring system (constraints, information gathering, safeguards) exceed even the costs of a culture in which dishonesty prevails. The cost explosion in the US health system is due to the enormous premiums doctors have to pay to insure themselves against malpractice suits. These costs are naturally passed on to patients. The head of a credit-card company told me that it spent millions on preventing credit card misuse, even though it would be cheaper simply to write off the losses.

The costs of developing, implementing and controlling financial incentive strategies (together with their disastrous side-effects). If I trust, I don't need to buy what I can get in any case: the willingness of my staff to work. Institutional motivation (bribery, reward, punishment) is no more than structural universal mistrust. Such systems don't even provide an opportunity to find out who is trustworthy. They encourage mutual deception because manipulation of the performance standard determines salary. As every field worker knows, there is nothing better than a bad previous year.

Taken together, these points argue that control should largely be replaced by trust, at least where control comes at a prohibitively high cost. But perhaps the best way to assess the value of trust is to ask what it costs to win back lost trust. Consider the British car industry. In the 1960s, wave after wave of redundancies had seriously damaged the relationship between companies and their staff, and the products were unreliable. The companies subsequently spared no efforts to restore their cars' reputation, but it took more than two decades. Today's car industry is half its former size, and not a single manufacturer remains in British ownership.

Because it produces staff loyalty and protects intrinsic motivation

There is a genetic basis for human nature, and it applies just as much to business management as it does to art or religion. Biology dictates that we thrive under some conditions and stagnate under others. All the psychological and sociological evidence shows that people flourish in an environment of trust.

We come close to this condition when we give a member of staff unfettered scope for action. The freedom to decide what to do stimulates interest and encourages people to take responsibility. It helps them feel engaged with their work – the motivation that comes from within. Trust increases the scope for nonconformity (the lateral thinking so highly regarded everywhere), individuality and originality. People can be who they are. Without trust, motivation doesn't last.

But trust doesn't just protect intrinsic motivation; it also binds staff to their company far more tightly than golden handcuffs ever could. Consider the research of Robert Levering, who conducts an opinion poll for *Fortune* magazine on the 100 best companies to work for in America, and who also invented the Levering Trust Index. The companies in the poll have an average trust index of 65 on a scale of 100; in other words, two-thirds of their staff say there is a distinctive climate of trust in their company. The companies outside the 100 best have a trust index of between 20 and 50 points, meaning that between 50 and 80 percent of their staff consider the level of trust in their company to be low. If we bear in mind that the number of unsolicited applications to the 100 best companies is up to 20 times that received by other companies, we can see that a high trust index represents a genuine competitive advantage in times when quality is scare in the labour market. Trust is a material asset in the endeavour to cultivate staff loyalty.

Because it makes management successful

Karin Müller, a committed teacher full of missionary zeal for new educational ideas, became head teacher of a primary school. Here was her chance to try out her ideas and give the school a new direction. She promoted her strategies with great conviction, brought in experts, distributed literature to colleagues and parents and began to introduce changes (the details of which I won't mention here in case they interfere with readers' impartiality). During the discussions, an authoritarian undertone crept into her arguments: anyone who didn't share her enthusiasm for new educational methods was damned as old-fashioned and provincial in their outlook. Her ideas were simply new and unfamiliar. Many of the teaching staff were sceptical; they felt their existing success wasn't appreciated. Some parents protested. The school had enjoyed a good reputation under the old principal, and the enrolment numbers had been high.

Karin Müller felt opposition brewing. She found she was obstructed in her mission to develop the most modern primary school in the district. She resorted to regulation: she decided to forbid her staff to discuss the school's teaching methods with parents. Instead, parents were invited to address problems and questions directly to her. Of course, this didn't stop the opposition; on the contrary, it strengthened it. Critical discussions continued; they simply took place without Karin Müller. Parents and teachers had known each other for a long time and had contact with each other outside the school.

Karin Müller trusted neither the parents nor her colleagues. Nor did she trust her powers of persuasion. Worst of all, she didn't trust her own ideas; if she had, she could have presented them in open discussion and defended them against criticism. She was dogmatic, unable to deal with resistance flexibly and in a way that maintained esteem for her opponents. What she brought about was mistrust, then resistance, followed by covert opposition and finally overt opposition. After three years of pain for all involved, she was transferred to another school.

Many studies have attempted to establish a correlation between internal company factors and corporate results. But only one variable has been substantiated as having a significant correlation: the nature of staff members' relationships with immediate managers. If the relationship is good, productivity increases; if it is bad, it declines. Within a relationship that someone experiences as positive, the most important feature is trust.

Again and again, I have seen managers achieve good results despite defying textbooks and making numerous management mistakes. I have met managers whom I found disagreeable but whose staff were evidently happy to follow them, and consequently they were successful. What's happening here confirms the results of research: there is a mix of factors that can't be neatly separated out, a combination of credibility, predictability and straightforwardness that we could sum up by the label "trust."

It has often been said that trust is the basis for management. Allowing oneself to be managed means trusting someone. In management seminars, this idea has often been brought to life by getting one participant to lead another around blindfolded.

Commitment and trust tend to go hand in hand. Trust is the only possible basis for communication, especially in the management model of personal responsibility, in which the person who is managed is regarded as a partner and intelligent supporter of company development, rather than just another hand on deck. Mutual dependence between partners entails eradicating the controlling elements of old management models.

If, for example, a director says he supports a member of his staff, two questions arise in the latter's mind: first, "Can I believe him?" second, "Is he interested in me?" The message of trust precedes the content of the message. It operates like a filter that determines whether the message is heard and believed. In some cases, directors can talk for hours without people paying attention to the content even for a minute. This is because trust is missing.

No manager can influence or lead people if he doesn't have trust. According to a study published recently, (the bibliographical reference for which I was not able to research but which I would nevertheless like to quote here) people are prepared to follow someone if they trust him, even if they don't share his views. But they won't follow if they share his views but don't trust him.

PepsiCo chairman Craig Weatherup said "People will tolerate honest mistakes, but if you violate their trust you will find it very difficult to ever regain their confidence. That is one reason that you need to treat trust as your most precious asset." General H. Norman Schwarzkopf put it well: "Leadership is a powerful mixture of strategy and trust. But if you have to get by without one of them, sacrifice strategy."

Trust will also help you out in difficult circumstances. If, for example, you can't keep an appointment or you do something that your staff find incomprehensible, they won't immediately assume you are being disloyal or betraying them. They will simply assume that something has gone wrong. If you have the trust of your staff, you'll also be able to change your mind without having to worry that you'll automatically be thought inconsistent or even untrustworthy. People will even excuse an occasional indiscretion, believing that it is an error on your part, or an exception. And if you do something that puts your staff at a disadvantage, they will credit you with the intention of preventing greater disadvantage. They may moan a bit, react without understanding, or even curse out loud – but if trust is there, such discord won't be serious. It will be seen as all part of the game. Trust is a durable, resilient position – "robust" as Fredmund Malik says.

The significance of trust becomes very clear in the fundamental management dilemma: the balancing act between the need to interfere and the need for acceptance. Managers have to interfere. They have to make sure their company is willing to change in order to protect itself from routines, complacency and the success trap. That can make them look awkward in the eyes of staff. On the other hand, managers can be effective only if they are recognized by the people they manage. They need the voluntary consent of their staff if they are to increase the value of the company over time. Only one quality can resolve this paradox: trust.

If trust is lacking, everything will be jinxed. The relationships between you and your staff will be like an equation that has a minus sign next to it. Everything will be reversed. Your most magnanimous gesture will be misunderstood; your staff will suspect you are up to something. Any initiative to build a positive relationship between management and staff will be regarded as a sophisticated form of manipulation. Nothing will work; every measure you take will fail. All you can do is end the co-operation.

A relationship of trust has two parties: the one who trusts and the one who is trusted. Ideally, trust should be mutual: each side trusts and each side is trusted. It is easier for staff; they have to trust only one person, the manager. But a manager usually has several staff. Many managers consider themselves trustworthy, but find trusting their staff difficult. This is understandable: trusting a lot of people isn't easy, and after all, you are responsible for the results.

Keeping control is getting more and more difficult. Hierarchical control and monitoring instruments are becoming less effective as employees' room for manoeuvre grows; staff have tasks that are becoming increasingly complex and less clearly defined. Companies with decentralized locations find cost-effective controlling activities impossible. Much is made of the possibilities of virtual co-operation, but the effective management of virtual teams calls for something quite different. Remote management – without regular or direct contact, without the possibility of talking face to face, having to include members in a common objective, to co-ordinate different interests and to do all this across multiple cultures and national borders – is impossible without trust.

The problem intensifies when highly qualified "brain workers" are managed. Such people have to organize their work for themselves to a large extent; often no one else can do it for them. Moreover, their productivity is not controllable; it can't be measured, it eludes quantification. What do they do when they work? They sit around! And if this weren't enough, many managers no longer understand the tasks of their staff. The head of research and development at a chemical company may hold a PhD in chemistry, but his staff may be recruited from dozens of disciplines, from pharmacology to biology and from molecular genetics to marketing. At best he may have an overview of their areas of work, but he certainly won't have expert knowledge. How else can he co-ordinate the work than through trust? Instead of formal systems that prevent evasion, he will need trust to ensure stability and co-ordination if staff are not to be suffocated.

The fact that trust bears the best fruits is demonstrated by informal working groups whose members are experts in a particular field and who engage in a common endeavour; the Linux software organization is an excellent example. Many companies already have knowledge networks independent of hierarchies. According to a 2001 estimate by Deloitte Consulting, there are 140 "com-

51

munities of practice" at DaimlerChrysler, 345 at Siemens, and 120 at the World Bank. As these virtual groups come together of their own accord and work without concrete assignments, their very existence shows that management have to place a high degree of trust in their staff.

So how do we manage staff whose output is difficult to quantify and whom we don't even see? By trusting them. Management exemplifies the two-way effect of trust and reveals that the reasons for trust are not only traditional, but also highly relevant to our present time.

WHAT IS TRUST?

There is no doubt that trust is a problematic concept. The word is used in such diverse contexts that it seems doubtful whether we can find a common denominator. In our modern society, trust even sounds a bit old-fashioned because modernization always means loss of trust. It is the price we pay for the differences in society, for the particular nature of subsystems.

My intention now is to explain precisely what trust is: in so doing, I want to advocate trust as a concept for the modern world and open the way for it to be practised. After all, if we don't know what trust is, we don't know what we can do to build it. Vague, undefined concepts invite misuse. They paralyze us. Only by defining a concept can we make it an instrument of cognition and prevent it from being used in an arbitrary way in moral arguments. By being conscious of misuse and getting rid of incorrect meanings, we can get closer to real understanding.

Where we encounter trust

Original trust

As human beings, we depend on each other. Who can grow up without being provided for and looked after? Who could feed and clothe themselves, make tools, formulate medicines and generate power without assistance from others? Who could make a telephone for their own use – and what would be the point? We all depend on others not only to exist but also to continue existing.

Trust is something we take for granted in dealing with things and people. It is familiar, a basic experience. When a newborn baby begins to distinguish itself from its environment, it has to learn to trust that the people who look after it will return. The psychologist Erik H. Erikson called this original trust. It is trust in the reliability of the world. We trust our own bodies; we believe that our hearts will continue beating, that wounds will heal, and that we will wake up after sleeping. We trust nature and the external world; we trust that spring will follow winter, that it will rain, that the earth will continue to turn. Our gods too are on the whole good-natured and reliable.

The basic trust between children and parents is probably the reason why there is always a heartfelt need for trust between people; this feeling exists on a deeper level than the rational intellect, and it never leaves us.

Trust as a social convention

Original trust is to be distinguished from trust as a *social convention*, a feature of modern societies. This trust trusts because it is customary, because it can't do otherwise, because it has to compensate for insufficient knowledge. Consider the things we consider to be true and rational. Most of them are things we aren't able to check for ourselves; we take them on the basis of our trust in other people. We rely on this trust, and on the chain of trust other people have in others. In the case of technology, we trust that the lift won't plunge to the bottom of the shaft, that the car will start, and that the fridge will work. If we buy a computer, we trust it will do what the sales assistant promised. We rely on goods and products we hardly understand created by people we don't know at places we've never visited.

We trust experts: you can't buy a house without legal help, you can't have your appendix removed without a doctor, and you couldn't install a software program if there were no IT specialists. And we trust the economy: we believe it will regulate the exchange of goods, create reasonably stable monetary value and facilitate a fair degree of market transparency. We trust the state to defend external borders, to protect us and to guarantee an independent judiciary. In a foreign city, we trust strangers to point us in the right direction rather than the wrong one. Even the structures of a company's organization represent trust in a system of formalized anticipated action. Trust manifests in long-established official channels, operational procedures, the permanent exchange of services, and expectations that managers will make decisions, staff will implement them and colleagues will co-operate.

You may be dubious about some of these examples. We all sense that trust has become brittle in many aspects of life; it is no longer unlimited. We don't have blind trust in our body (otherwise we wouldn't go to the doctor), in nature (otherwise we wouldn't set up water storage systems), in the state (otherwise there would be no separation of powers) or in the economy (otherwise there would be no Monopolies Commission). We don't have blind trust in technology (otherwise there would be no warranties) or in experts (otherwise we wouldn't obtain second opinions). On closer examination, trust appears to be a paradise from which we have long been banished.

Trust as competence

For the British sociologist Anthony Giddens, modern societies are characterized by uprooting. Our living conditions have been separated from their local context and restructured across time and space. We can't control the sources of our food supplies; we haven't assembled the aircraft that will carry us over the Atlantic; the job market isn't confined to our local district. More and more people purchase goods by telephone or via the internet, trusting the person at the other end to dispatch the goods they have paid for. Displacement also applies to our fellow human beings: trust can seldom develop organically out of long-standing acquaintance. Most people we deal with in everyday life are people we don't know.

A new form of trust needs to be introduced here: a trust that is competence. This trust knows all about the world's dangers and people's unreliability. It is aware that people all too often break agreements and act irresponsibly. It calculates the risk. It is prepared to take this risk and nevertheless work on the assumption that conditions are predictable and people are trustworthy.

To the exact extent that trust is a risk, it becomes a *personal contribution*. It has to compensate for the impossibility of having everything under control. It has to overcome fear. It has to make up for our lack of knowledge and familiarity. That is why trust is fundamental to the modern age. It marks the transition from tradition to the present day as nothing else does.

Trust as decision

Modern trust is based on people's having chosen to work together and trust each other. This trust is reflective and calculating. This trust is neither blind nor naïve. This trust is a decision.

And it is diametrically opposed to the ordinary understanding that trust grows slowly and is a reward for which the other person needs to have worked for a long time. We say "This person has never let me down yet," by which we mean "Trust has to be earned." It's the same in companies: a new person is regarded with suspicion for a long time, especially in companies where the mentality of "I don't care what happens after I've left" rules in job rotations.

In my view, the idea that trust can be based only on sustained positive experience is neither necessary nor forward-looking.

Not necessary. The most creative co-operation is probably based on intensive short-term trust. Musicians who come together for sessions are a good example. When it works – and I have seen it happen several times – the experience is unforgettable. The film industry is another example. When a crew comes together, few of the members know each other, but by working intensely together for a few weeks they develop trust extremely quickly. This happens because they know their co-operative relationship is built around this project alone, with a clearly defined objective and a common journey in which each person has a specific role to play.

Not forward-looking. We can't hope to compensate for our modern lack of trust by returning to nostalgic old sources of trust. A long-term orientation, a sense of community, good intentions and moral obligations: these are important values, but they work only in exceptional cases. Film crews' ability to develop trust without familiarity is precisely what's needed in companies that have to adapt quickly to changing markets. If we are to keep pace with the speed of the modern world, we have to put trust on a new footing. The old trust was characterized by the fact that it didn't derive from an explicit decision; its effect wasn't identified. The type of trust required now is based on a conscious decision, and recognizes the possibility of disappointment.

Under current economic conditions, then, we can't easily avoid the responsibility to relate to *trust as a choice*. With regard to management, I can only agree with Carolyn Dyer, senior analyst at Gallup, when she says "The best managers trust their people from the first day. On the basis of an inner conviction they trust them to do their best and to deliver good work. Only the cynical managers think staff have to earn trust first." I'm also grateful to my first manager for a more or less casual remark that I didn't at first understand; I made a note of it and have carried it with me ever since: "People have to earn my mistrust."

Trust in co-operation

When we trust, we assume that the other person will generally act with goodwill, has the best intentions, doesn't wish us any harm, and gives us nothing to fear. We can count on them; we know they will be there when we need them. We relax and feel secure. Our life is in any case incompatible with the idea that, as Jürgen Habermas put it, "Everything could be quite different at any time." This is the general understanding of trust. To help us in the quest for a useful definition, I have chosen a situation we are all familiar with: a visit to the hairdresser.

Imagine you are on holiday in a foreign city and want to go to a hairdresser. This is a person you don't know, yet you will allow them to come into close physical proximity in a way that would normally be appropriate only for your doctor. And your looks are at stake! You have some time, so you wander the streets and look at various salons. What will be your selection criteria? Whom are you going to trust? You take a risk when you sit in that chair. You have to invest trust in advance.

But the same applies to the hairdresser. If he accepts you as a customer, he trusts you will pay for his work afterwards; he has faith in your intention and ability to pay. He can tell you are a tourist, and he'll work out whether he's going to put himself out. He'll probably never see you again, but perhaps his professional honour won't allow him to do bad work. And he never knows, you might decide to stay after all, and if you're satisfied you may provide a welcome bit of additional income.

Now you've made your decision: you enter the salon, sit down and watch the hairdresser work. The way he moves, the way he advises you, the way the salon looks: all this helps you to develop a sense of trust, or at least confidence. While the hairdresser is cutting your hair, your trust may waver: he's cutting in a different way from your usual hairdresser. But you can see he is engaged in the work, concentrating hard. Then you see the result: it looks different, but it's actually quite impressive, it's a refreshing change. You like the way you look. You find your trust confirmed. You are relieved. You pay with a sense of satisfaction, and you are genuinely happy: about the new hairstyle? The confirmed trust? The successful gamble? The hairdresser too sees his trust confirmed, and he's pleased that you're pleased (he's pleased with the tip as well), and he says goodbye in a warm and friendly tone.

When you leave, you consider returning at the end of your vacation. The hairdresser has taken you seriously as a customer, even though you're a tourist. In any case, you'll pay another visit next time you are on vacation there. Your trust is strengthened by the fact that he did not exploit it.

Both the essential components of the concept of trust in co-operation emerge from this example: interaction and uncertain behaviour.

Reciprocity. Reciprocity is characteristic of co-operation because the objectives of one partner can be achieved only with the help of the other partner. Cut your hair yourself and you might turn out as a visual blight. And without customers whose hair keeps grow-

59

ing, hairdressers will soon become (as they used to be) something between a doctor and a bartender.

Uncertain behaviour. Uncertain behaviour occurs in co-operation when the partners have some degree of choice in their actions. Risk arises because you can't be certain that the other person will do what you want him to. He can choose, but you don't know what his choice will be. He is free. Trust is therefore an opportunity to form a relationship with the other person's freedom.

Niklas Luhmann puts it like this: trust is a potential solution for problems involving risk. Accordingly, trust presupposes a risk situation. Risk comes first. Then comes trust (or mistrust). Carefully considered trust doesn't therefore constitute risk taking, despite what is claimed in much of the literature: if that were so, then mistrust would logically also be a risky inaction taken in advance, which is obviously nonsense. The dividing line is different. The risky situation, which may turn out one way or the other, confronts you with the choice of trusting or mistrusting. It is not trust *itself* that is the risk. The risk remains: it neither increases nor decreases, regardless of your decision.

When does risk arise?

* When you don't know the other person
* When you don't know whether he is able or willing
* When there is a time delay before the recompense.

Not knowing someone. The hairdresser example represents a situation that more and more people encounter every day. They don't know the other person. They have no experience of him or her. In modern business life, we are witnessing the disappearance of a trust based on conservative conventions that people take for granted and that continue for a long time. The more discontinuous and fluid our encounters are in the business world, the more difficult it is to build trust on the basis of a common history. In a global economy with ever-faster technological development, we seldom experience close, long-term co-operative conditions. We are much quicker than before to change partners, suppliers and companies, and our colleagues hardly ever remain with us for the whole of our working lives. The more mobile and short-term the co-operation, the greater the need for trust.

However, occupational mobility doesn't just mean changes in jobs. Changes in location are often unavoidable, and make it hard to maintain long-term friendships and connections. People who keep having to start again have no prior experience of the people they meet. There is no common history – the traditional basis for trust. There is a danger of social uprooting.

In the course of mechanization and globalization, the basis for trust has changed. Trust no longer has the quality of "This is how it has always been." It is no longer simply one quality among others. But most people are lagging behind this development at an emotional level. They can't grow at the speed they need to in order to co-operate with strangers. This is expressed in such comments as "It's impossible to build trust with all this restructuring" and "I have a new manager every other month. Last year there were six." But if we have no personal or shared life experience, if we can't build up a common history as background security (Niklas Luhmann), we'll have to build trust in a different way.

Not knowing whether someone is able or willing. If you trust, you allow another person to take care of something important. In the hairdresser example, it's your appearance. There is scope for discretion within this care. You can't be sure that the hairdresser shares your aesthetic taste. You can't be sure that a good haircut means the same thing to both of you. You can't even be certain he will do what you have both agreed. We can never fully know another person; we can't see into him, and his private intentions aren't accessible to us. The hairdresser may, for example, not make much effort; he may be lacking *willingness* to work.

Would mistrust have been a better response to the risk, then? Not at all: if his lack of willingness to work was just a freak occurrence on that particular day and you distrust him from now on, you may miss out on a brilliant haircut that you would be delighted with next time. What if his lack of willingness is based on bad experiences with tourists in the past? In that case, your positive response to the new haircut can overturn his prejudice at a stroke.

It could be that the hairdresser wants to give you a wonderful hairstyle, but isn't *capable* of it. In that case, he lacks the *ability* to do the job. You may be able to work out whether he is good at his job by watching him. But in the end you can't be certain. Trust is based on give and take. How would you have fared, where would you be today, if the first customer you dealt with had said "I'm not going to work with him. He looks too young and inexperienced. The risk is too high"?

Time delay before recompense. Markets are characterized by a balance between giving and receiving. The weekly market I visited with my mother throughout my childhood was an example. Goods for money. Immediately. Some transactions involve delay and are carried out step by step. In the hairdresser example, the exchange follows without major delay. The hairdresser cuts your hair and *then* you pay. But you could rush out without paying, or sue the hairdresser for injury. Service and payment don't always have to be *simultaneous.* In relationships with a future – those in which there is an intention of long-term co-operation – there may be a substantial time gap between provision of goods or services and eventual payment. An example is mail order: the company sends the goods and receives payment a few weeks later. Or an employee works hard and contributes a lot now in the expectation of being promoted in a few years' time. Partners' contributions don't have to offset one another immediately in every exchange transaction, but rather over the course of a relationship based on exchange. This involves risk. Recompense may not be forthcoming.

However, the risk applies to both partners. Uncertainty is mutual. If each partner's behaviour depends on the other's, no exchange can take place. Nothing happens. That's the moment of *decision*. In such situations you can decide to trust or distrust. It's a situation of uncertainty, an intermediate state between knowing and not knowing (Georg Simmel), an interval in which the decision may go one way or the other.

Following these preliminary considerations, I want to define trust as follows:

I am prepared to relinquish control of another person because I expect them to be competent, and to act with integrity and goodwill.

Practising trust therefore means considering the possibility of betrayal. To trust means not believing that betrayal will occur. Betrayal is possible, but unlikely. Trust is the expectation that co-operative action won't be exploited. It enables us to act under conditions of co-operation and uncertainty.

Limits of trust

"Jesus – My trust is in Thee." The sticker is displayed so prominently on the back of the car that you can't miss it. I don't feel comfortable when I see this type of public declaration. There's something unwholesome about it. That aside, what does it say? What is being communicated here? That the driver feels safe? That his moves are guided from above? That eternal life is waiting? All these things?

Similarly, "Don't trust anyone over 30," "Cash is the only thing you can trust," "You can't trust management." Such generalizations may derive from long experience and be understandable in individual cases, but in terms of content they are *empty*. At this level, trust is a woolly platitude. It refers to everything and nothing. It calls for closer definition. In what respect do I trust someone?

For some years now, a company at my local airport has been offering to look after cars while drivers go away. When they return, their car is clean and its petrol tank is full. Whenever I go there, the same man always greets me in a friendly way. Every time I give him my car keys and he drives my car to a remote car park. I've known the man for years, and yet I don't actually know him. I don't know where he lives, how he lives, what he does in his spare time, whether he has esoteric hobbies, or even whether he is a criminal. But every time I give him the keys. So far, the car has always been ready on time, clean and undamaged.

The trust I place in this man is a specific trust concentrated on a specific action. Unlike the Jesus example, it doesn't extend to all areas of life. Take the case of an employee who is brilliant at solving problems but not much good at customer contact. Or who is bubbling over with new ideas but doesn't keep appointments or attend meetings punctually. Our trust in the hairdresser is equally specific. On the other hand, the trust I have in my friend Peter, whom I have known for over 40 years, is unspecific, and yet it has limits: for example, I wouldn't trust him to repair my laptop. Someone may be honest, upright, predictable and *willing* to work, but is he also competent, experienced, knowledgeable and *able* to work? In some respects, I trust people I don't know more than I trust my friend. It is only sensible that trust is always *limited*.

We trust in different ways in different contexts. Trust is usually limited to a particular area that it doesn't extend beyond. This is the way it has to be: someone's terrible behaviour is often the search for a limit that they can respect.

Is this limited trust then mistrust? In order to answer this question, I'm going to deal with principles again.

Trust as "either/or"

We aren't usually aware of the fact that we trust someone. We take it for granted. If people whom we trust behave as we expect, we barely notice. We live with a vague awareness of things, and we don't know how things are going to develop. This is the reason we often undervalue trust. We aren't aware of it until it has been broken. Then we are usually astonished, sometimes even shocked. Those who have lost trust in a friend will have the clearest understanding of what trust is.

Trust is often defined as something pre-conscious: as long as we have trust, we aren't aware of it. Trust is inconspicuously self-evident. We become aware of it only when it has been betrayed. Starting from this premise, we could never say "I trust you," only "I trusted you." Some authors therefore assume that conscious trust is no longer real trust. The question "Can I trust them or not?" already marks a shift in the direction of mistrust. According to this view, trust is a condition that can only deteriorate; a precarious, fleeting state of mind.

We become aware of trust only once it is lost – or more accurately, when it has started to fade. Then we use terms such as "hope" or "confidence" instead. Some may think this is mere wordplay. What's true is that undiminished trust can barely exist for a modern adult. There is no way back into the paradise of immediacy. A person who has recognized trust has been infected by mistrust. Once awakened, doubt can never be dismissed.

Either/or: this is one of the greatest obstacles on the path to recognizing trust as the elixir of life in the business world. What's missing is a sensible intermediate position. But if I want to talk about trust, build trust and make a decision about trust, I have to be aware of it. Only then does it become an option I can choose. In the following discussion I shall therefore start from the premise that only conscious trust is real trust: the conviction that the other person won't betray me, although I know they could. I shall leave it to you to judge whether "hope" or "confidence" might be better terms for this. What's important to me is that the diminution of trust is a condition for its very existence.

It is worth taking time to think about these ideas.

Trust versus mistrust

People tend to develop "categorical systems" (R. Reinhold) for themselves and their understanding of the world to help them create order. Trust versus mistrust is a concept that has been used for countless years. This categorical distinction leads people to think in mutually exclusive alternatives, going from one extreme to the other. Trust is an idea that stands in irreconcilable contrast to the idea of mistrust. This is also the background to the common belief in either/or: "Trust is either there or not." "Trust has to be total. Either I trust you or I don't. There's nothing in between." Seen from this perspective, trust is *unconditional*, not linked to any conditions. This trust is once and for all, and exists either as an unshakeable foundation or not at all.

This view of trust is one that seems to be imposed by certain experiences. But it's possible to misinterpret experiences once you have settled on a particular view of trust. (We are approaching a wide-open mental trap here, into which many a hot-headed disputant has fallen.) Even if it appears profoundly counterintuitive to some people, trust is *linked to conditions* in the same way that freedom can't exist without limits (otherwise the concept of freedom would be empty because we wouldn't be able to make any statements about it). If we describe these conditions as "mistrust," we are making a verbal prejudgement that immediately suggests a moral judgement. This makes us pull back; who would want to be considered mistrustful?

Any idea requires limits. This also applies to trust. Everything we value as trust can be attained only *within a framework* of knowledge and *in conditions of* relative security. Because knowledge is limited and total security isn't possible, we must complement both with trust. Knowledge and security don't necessarily amount to mistrust; they are the basis to which trust can relate. This means that knowledge is the *primary idea* that must be in place before we can speak about trust. Trust and mistrust don't represent a contradiction; they are interrelated in a flowing equilibrium. We must find a measure to establish a position between two seemingly pathological [*?] poles. We must decide what this measure is to be.

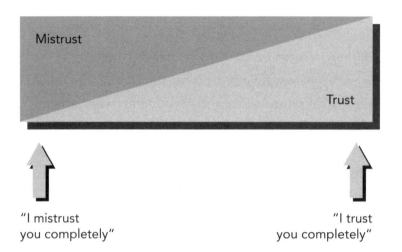

Mistrust

Trust

"I mistrust
you completely"

"I trust
you completely"

We need to be aware that trust is a strong word. Most attempts at a definition play trust off against the weaker concept of control. But that too is open to misunderstanding.

Trust versus control

Walt Disney was a person with an almost obsessive need for control. He was notorious for prowling alone at night through the deserted offices of his cartoonists to check on their daily output. Yet in some ways his studio had a more relaxed regime than others: there was no clocking-in, for instance. Nor were staff expected to produce a set number of drawings. On the contrary, Disney encouraged them to be self-critical and to throw away any pieces of work with which they weren't happy. In this way, he successfully balanced control and trust within his company. The fact that his employees obviously felt well treated speaks in his favour.

Control is something unpleasant; at least, the term isn't overly popular. Control is accepted, but people don't like it and find it annoying. It's often dressed up as something more palatable, going under the name of feedback, variation analysis, benchmarking, reviews or flexitime. Controllers whose job it is to safeguard efficiency on behalf of management have pointed out for decades that their job title takes a capital "C." One often reads that controlling isn't compatible with modern management. Learning, innovation and a culture of trust are supposed to be the order of the day. On the other hand, the fear of losing control is rising as business boundaries blur and market dynamics speed up. What people tend to forget is that learning can't take place if the outcome isn't monitored.

Trust and control – here seen as a comparison between what's desirable and what's real – are not contradictory concepts. Without normative guidelines, our lives would be impossible. Trust without control is inconceivable. Control is the condition for trust, the basis on which it can be built. Control is a prerequisite for trust to function. The question we may need to discuss is this: how great is the *measure* of trust? Trust is not a fixed quantity, irrespective of context. Trust is a *relational term* that denotes a greater or lesser level.

What becomes clear from the above is that control doesn't necessarily undermine trust. Control can actually *safeguard* trust. The higher the degree of trust, the more important the safeguarding function of control. It then acquires an informative, supporting and enhancing character. But if on the other hand trust is displaced beyond a certain threshold, the experience becomes one of mistrust. The higher the degree of mistrust, the more limiting control becomes, thereby diminishing trust still further. "If he doesn't trust me," the employee will think, "why should I take his interests into account?" The threshold differs from company to company, from situation to situation, from task to task, from employee to employee. How much is too little, and how much is too much? The optimum ratio between trust and control is not constant, but will fluctuate according to the situation and the occasion.

Few will object to the suggestion of a well-known school of management, "Trust everybody as far as you can – and go right up to the limit," because it doesn't make any precise statement. What would be too far? Up to which limit? But if the following statement is take as an elaboration: "But make sure you find out whenever your trust has been abused" there is ample scope for misunderstanding. It's difficult to know quite what is meant by trust when terms like "make sure," "whenever" and "abused" are brought in. When these ideas are illustrated by examples from child-rearing, the author can count on the approval of all those who cling to the past, since he is invoking the conventional educational wisdom that has been poisoning thinking on the management of adults for decades.

All young auditors have had "Trust is good, control is better" imprinted on their brain. Attributed to Lenin, the phrase is a constant invitation to the either/or way of thinking. However, the Russian Academy for Language and Poetry tells us that this sentence goes back to another saying often quoted by Lenin: "Trust, but control as well." This means something different. It points to the *complementary* use of trust and control. It aims at a type of trust that doesn't want to dispense with control altogether. This view doesn't play off trust against control; it is softer, promotes the idea of working together and divides tasks into those that should be underpinned by control and those that should be managed by trust. You can be both trusting *and* vigilant. Ronald Reagan, who no doubt made a great contribution to the end of the Cold War, knew this: "Trust but verify."

To some extent, contracts seem to represent the antithesis of trust. Why enter into a contract to protect your interests if you trust someone? But contracts can provide a platform on which a trusting collaboration can be built. Take an employment contract. If it regulates the essentials and confines itself to the minimum, it will never see the light of day again once an employee has started work. But without it, many would never start at all. It represents a minimum guarantee for mutually acceptable behaviour. No more, but no less either. In the case of agreements on targets or projects, it is advisable to have regular joint reviews. Here, control means keeping people updated and informed, making an investment in co-operation as an active partnership that is being taken seriously. "Are things going as planned? Do we still share a common understanding of the agreement we made?"

These considerations illustrate what those who strive for trust in practice know already: the subject invites extremes. People often alternate between Grand Hotel Abyss and Villa Sunshine. Trust is generally seen as good and mistrust as bad in the softened version of control as better. Or vice versa, depending on your view of the world. Trusting people are seen immediately as credulous, chummy or lacking distance; their opposites are labelled control freaks. A manager who doesn't constantly check up on subordinates is regarded as acting recklessly. And a person who checks out agreements is judged mistrustful. Let me state it clearly once more: checking out an agreement doesn't indicate mistrust. It's wrong to set trust and control against one another. They aren't mutually exclusive, but rather mutually *dependent*. Trust isn't possible without control, nor control without trust. It is the proportion that is important.

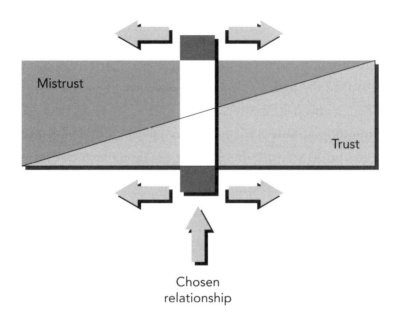

Mistrust

Trust

Chosen
relationship

Blind trust, blind mistrust

The Brazilian Ayrton Senna, one of the most successful Formula One drivers of all time, possessed a deep-rooted religious faith that gave him a sense of total security. "Because of his trust in God, Senna thought he was invulnerable," says his former team mate Alain Prost. "As a result he drove faster than anybody else." A deceptive security: Senna died on 1 May 1994 at the notorious Tamburello bend at Imola. People with an idealistic (non-pragmatic) willingness to trust have a tendency to trust themselves and others too much. They invest excessive trust in someone whom they consider almighty. Paradoxically, the carbon-fibre monocoques currently used in Formula One racing have the same fatal effect as Senna's trust in God: they make some drivers feel invulnerable and drive recklessly. When cockpits were made of cast aluminium, with unprotected fuel tanks that turned them into bombs on wheels, drivers were aware of the risks they ran. "It made us act defensively at the start," says former driver Jacques Laffite, "We were fully aware of the danger."

Trust shouldn't mean jettisoning caution, safeguards and controls. No limitation can be greater than that of a total lack of limits. Those who go to extremes can prove only that nothing works. It isn't a matter of trust versus mistrust or either/or, but a matter of more of one and less of the other. This book is a search for a plausible proportion of the exaggerated and the non-exaggerated.

In other words, we need to make a distinction. Different circumstances and tasks call for different levels of trust. We always trust in relation to something, never blindly. *Trust mustn't be blind*, whether at the beginning or during the course of a collaboration. At the beginning, the undifferentiated blind trust of the credulous philanthropist is worthless because it doesn't differentiate. It doesn't take into account the possibility of disappointment, and therefore doesn't honour the other party as being worthy of trust.

Blind trust is more likely to reduce people's willingness to trust than to increase it (witness the mass suicides of sect members). It can even be an incentive to fraud. For this reason, you'll always experience deception and disappointment in connection with blind trust. In its extreme form, trust paradoxically destroys the basis for its own future. A certain measure of selective mistrust is required in order to give worth to trust and to ensure its continued existence.

The same applies to the continued existence of a collaboration. Trust is like an advance: it can be cashed in later. Trust is always on trial. To be sure, if you as a manager constantly look over your employee's shoulder to make sure everything is going according to plan, acting as if you are engaged in some sort of permanent strategic reconnaissance mission, it will be taken as a clear sign of mistrust. But if you work together for any length of time, trust still needs to be justified by results now and again if it is to be continually renewed. That's what sets it apart from the rule of obedience or loyalty to the alliance that still dominates many businesses today. If your interests are upheld by the other person's actions in the expected manner, your trust remains intact.

However, blind trust is the least of our worries. It rarely occurs in business; blind mistrust is much more likely to be the problem. A concept that might seem funny when displayed in a shop window – "In God we trust; all others pay cash" – acts as a brake on a business's future development when it sums up the attitude of much of the management. There's a danger of falling into the trap of mistrust when we are paralyzed by our fear of risk and no longer ask ourselves whether we might not endanger our economic survival through thoughtless safety measures. Trust brings risk with it, but so does mistrust. There is no business without risk.

Many perfectionists fall into this trap. They are idealistic people who trust no one but themselves to do a job properly. They prefer to do everything themselves, whatever the cost. They always find fault with other people's performance. To them, other people are intrinsically less able. They won't be budged from their conviction that there's always a single best solution to any problem. An approximation, an imprecise but practicable solution, is unthinkable. To put it bluntly: perfectionists aren't capable of trust; nor are they capable of *co-operation* in its strict sense.

Let me put it in figures. Let's assume it's possible to control the behaviour of another person 100 percent. We have two extreme scenarios to chose from: 100 percent trust ("I trust you completely") and 100 percent mistrust ("I mistrust you completely"). Beyond this 100 percent lies the range of blind trust ("I trust everybody") or the range of blind mistrust ("I mistrust everybody").

When we're in a position to evaluate the *relative* trustworthiness of someone, we're dealing with a proportion. And it is this proportion that we need to make a decision on. The decision will differ depending on the situation, the context, the consequences and so on. And it is open to change. If I invest a higher degree of trust in a collaborative relationship, I shift that relationship to the right. If I do the opposite, I shift it to the left.

Trust must remain constructive; it mustn't make you blind and mustn't ever be absolute. The same goes for mistrust. Trusting everybody is a mistake; so is trusting nobody. Just as it's possible to trust too little, it's also possible to trust too much. Do that and you are easy prey; do the other and you lead a miserable life. At the end, Hitler trusted no one but his dog.

Modern trust therefore involves a decision in favour of a combination of trust and mistrust, of control and the relinquishing of control.

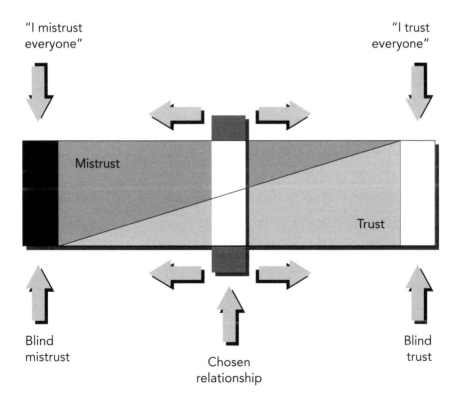

But what are the correct proportions? Is my trust naïve? Is it a stubborn refusal to consider the risks and implications of any betrayal? That depends on the consequences you consider, because all actions are linked in a structure of interconnecting parts. When the decisions behind these actions are made, they focus on certain possibilities and neglect others. But these others are just as valid, and might even be considered as more important by someone else. You can always adopt a perspective from which someone else's actions can be considered naïve.

Managers tend to trust too little rather than too much. Those who wish to change this situation and take small steps towards trust often feel they are losing control altogether. They feel they are letting go of the reins and surrendering themselves to the other direction, although in reality they are only loosening the reins a little. They want to be seen as trustworthy and usually believe they are, yet they don't want to be regarded as trusting unduly. But because there is always a perspective from which trust, however justified, can be judged to be blind, they protect themselves so as to be able to justify their actions.

Misunderstandings about trust

Earlier I said that trust is *not* something that you have to earn over a period of time. At this point, I'd like to go into other misunderstandings about the nature of trust in a little more detail.

Trust as something good

Discussions about trust almost always include assumptions about outdated concepts of virtue. Henry David Thoreau said: "A noble person cannot give a greater gift than his whole trust; no other gift enhances the giver and the recipient so much." Well said. Trust is often weighty, moralistic, admonishing. The question "Don't you trust me?" makes you eager to say you do. Trust is often viewed as an unalloyed substance like honey, spreading well-being wherever it flows.

But this picture is skewed. Trust isn't intrinsically good. There are immoral trusting relationships as well as moral ones. Mafia members have a strong sense of professional honour. The Hawala banking system, which I praised earlier for its speed, acts as an insuperable obstacle to Western intelligence organizations in their efforts to stem financial support for terrorism. The American scientist Annette Baier called criminals the real experts in trust. And we can all imagine circumstances in which destroying trust could be morally justified.

In some cases, defensive managers misuse trust as a label. They don't pay attention, don't act, don't manage, and excuse their passivity by claiming trust in their employees. But trust can never mean retreat and passivity. Once again, there is a fine line between taking too much and too little responsibility.

We have all experienced situations where we are taken into someone's trust. Gossip is an example of such a trust ritual. You show trust because you are sure the person you confide in won't make use of your confidences. But such trust is often abused as a sort of communication currency. Someone offers up information that they have obtained under the seal of secrecy in order to worm their way into the confidence of a third person. They defame the absent person in order to ingratiate themselves with those present. They sacrifice trust on the altar of relationship building in order to obtain an *ad hoc* advantage. Is that moral?

The fact that trust doesn't necessarily have to be linked to a stable moral concept emerges from the results of the World Value Survey, a survey devised by a team of economists from the universities of Harvard and Chicago in order to determine the measure of trust within a society. They found that the highest levels of trust are to be found in Scandinavia, where two-thirds of respondents agreed with the statement that you can trust strangers. The lowest values were found in countries with hierarchical religions.

We shouldn't let our thinking be confined by a tendency to moralize. Total immersion in any all-consuming idea tends to distort our judgement. Trust is neither good nor bad. There is no need to evaluate it at all. It can be explained more or less fully as a product of rational deliberation with no moral component. But more on that later.

Trust as feeling

Feelings account for a significant part of our biological makeup. Their origins, function and meaning are disputed, in particular their difficult relationship with the unerring eye of reason. Some consider that emotions interfere with rationality; others block any reasoned argument by retreating behind their feelings. Yet others laud a vague concept of emotional intelligence as a way out of the dead end.

Trust has been drawn into the maelstrom of this dispute. Khalil Gilbran, who is often inappropriately thought of as an author of aphorisms, writes: "Trust is an oasis of the heart, which is never reached by the caravan of thought." That sounds compelling in its eloquence. The same idea is expressed by Eveline in André Gide's novel *The School for Wives*; she speaks of her emerging doubts about the trustworthiness of her husband Robert: "I only felt instinctively that there was something indefinable there, which sounded wrong." It can't be expressed any better: "felt instinctively . . . something indefinable." But the same applies to the financial markets too. This is what the *Frankfurter Allgemeine Zeitung* had to say in October 2000: "It is not that the Japanese electronics group Sony has ever had a lack of vision. Both in the area of new products and new strategies, the group has always been successful in playing the role of innovator ahead of the game. But although Sony continues to conquer the market with new products, investors' trust in the brand has been declining for months." The term "stock market psychology" has come to be used to refer to the component of feeling involved here.

In the end, the same applies to the relationship between manager and employee. Whatever the rationale for an enhanced relationship of trust ("Trust pays!"), it will be hindered by the fact that companies are not enterprises of pure economic rationality. If someone doesn't want to trust, nothing will happen. Of course, that person will hardly ever own up; we can always find "rational" reasons not to trust that we can use to explain our emotional resistance.

Reason alone isn't sufficient to make a decision for or against trust. Emotion always plays a part too. Most people will agree that trust comes from the gut. It follows that creating a climate of trust is not simply a matter of adopting rational, controlled behaviour; fostering co-operation between people also entails unconscious communication such as the detection and interpretation of "I trust you" signals. The climate of trust and the more subtle associated behaviour traits can't usually be created directly, but often develop naturally from empathy. Although trust can't be generated merely by an act of will, it is possible to practise trust and to develop towards it. A trusting person sends inconspicuous signals to others that would be virtually impossible to reproduce intentionally in their entirety and complexity. These signals may cause the recipient to reward the sender for his or her trust. This means that in the case of a positive outcome, the participants are both doing the right thing on the basis not only of rational calculation, but also of their felt sense. I for one wouldn't know how my evaluation of someone else's trustworthiness could develop unless my feelings were involved in some way.

Consequently, it is useful to watch other people's behaviour closely. Look and see who you trust. Not many people can control their body language so consistently that they can sham the feelings that genuine interaction is based on. "Look more and hope less."

The best way to show what is actually there as regards your own involuntary behaviour is undoubtedly not to try and act a part. You should ask yourself: do I want to trust the other person? To them, mere verbal affirmations without a deep inner conviction will look disingenuous, and prevent precisely what they aim to achieve. It's a matter of being genuine. Especially where complex decisions are involved, we should use our intuitive judgement instead of searching for other means to achieve an objectivity that will in any case lack credibility in the end.

How does intuition work? Whether we trust someone at first sight depends on a variety of indistinct impressions. We see someone, and from their behaviour, their clothes, the sound of their voice, their facial expression (especially their eyes), we develop ideas of who this person is. We normally call this our intuition. We use the imprecise term "intuition" because we can't (or don't want to) articulate the basic data (aspects of perception and standards) that underlie our emotions. We generally underestimate how quickly we judge someone's trustworthiness. Prejudices and generalizations as well as past experiences influence the process. You might trust a tradesman more than a scientist, a country dweller more than a town person, a woman more than a man, or *vice versa*.

People do make mistakes, as everyone knows. After meeting Joseph Stalin, H. G. Wells opined: "Never met a man more candid, fair and honest.... no one is afraid of him and everybody trusts him." A good feeling isn't an adequate basis for trust.

But I have another point to make here: trust needs to be talked about. If feelings are to be acknowledged as influencing our judgement, they need to be accessible to justification and refutation, as all judgements are. We mustn't hide behind them. They need to be discussed so that reason is placed alongside emotion, especially if you are keen on *creating* trust. This is what I will turn to next when we look at trust in practice. If we simply go with our feelings, we remain powerless and must accept what is or is not. If we wish to shape the present, we can improve the conditions that make trust possible. We can't force another person to trust us, but we can increase the likelihood that they will. But only those who already feel what I am about to explain will appreciate that.

HOW DO I SHOW TRUST?

What can you do to make another person trust you? At first glance, trust appears to be a state that can't be brought about actively. Whether another person trusts you is something you can't influence or control. Reliability, consistency, predictability, keeping promises, fairness, loyalty, honesty, discretion, credibility: these are certainly important in terms of *maintaining* trust. But what causes trust to *arise*?

Myth: Trust-building measures

If someone refuses to trust you, you have no choice but to accept it. All the same, the literature is full of suggestions about what a manager can do to create trust. Most of the trust-building measures I have come across are well meant, but weak and ineffective. Some are trite and futile. They all ignore the hierarchical conditions under which they are supposed to be effective. Let's have a look at some of them so that you don't stumble into a trap, albeit with the best intentions.

Asking for trust

When we run out of arguments, when we can't convince people, when we decide that something mustn't be spoken about in public, we ask for trust. But does the person who asks for trust earn it? Doesn't asking for trust invite the very thing that trust is supposed to overcome, namely mistrust? Someone who asks for something usually wants to sell something; he accentuates the positive and plays down the negative. We sense we aren't getting the whole truth. What we took for granted is undermined by the imploring speech. When trust wanes, people sometimes react by making an appeal that actually drives away the very thing they are advocating. Someone who exposed a member of staff yesterday won't succeed in recreating a trusting relationship tomorrow even if he asks for trust.

When mistrust has arisen, there will be reasons. Simply saying "Trust me" doesn't deal with these reasons; it may even cause resistance. It ignores the reasons and exploits the positive associations of trust to push the sceptical party into the territory of moral bankruptcy. Someone who says "Trust me" is effectively declaring trust to be a debt the other person owes them. The subtext is: "…if you don't trust me, there's something wrong with you." In fact, when people are told "Trust me" they often feel ashamed or guilty if they don't manage to trust. When we don't trust, we are implicitly accused of not having the right attitude. People tell us what we should feel, but what we really feel is that there are reasons for our distrust. Too little is offered; too much is demanded.

"Trust me" is a highly manipulative communication technique. Some success trainers present themselves as role models: "Look at me! I've done it!" Some managers deal with critical questions by saying "I can't talk about it at the moment. I have to ask you to trust me." Often this is a pretext to avoid having to explain motives and actions or to face legitimate arguments. People don't like being criticized. If the other person still insists on pursuing their question, their lack of trust can be highlighted, which effectively knocks them off their base of moral decency. Rhetoric is used to depict the legitimate wish to understand as morally deplorable. Trust can be used as a protective weapon: "You are a bad person if you don't trust me."

You don't build trust by talking about it. Quite the opposite: "Trust me" has the same disastrous effect on trust as sunlight has on a vampire. It evaporates when it is made into a theme in that way. You are more trustworthy when you don't ask people for trust.

Be straightforward

Is your behaviour consistent and predictable? If it is confusing and inconsistent, people will find it difficult to trust you. "Today I do this, tomorrow I do that" is disastrous to a trusting relationship. Your staff must be able to count on you acting consistently in comparable situations, or at least, that's the popular view. And I must say, when I encounter managers whom people trust, they almost always seem straightforward and predictable. It seems to me that straightforward and predictable behaviour is a necessary condition for trust. But is it sufficient in order to create trust?

Straightforwardness is particularly difficult in management. How are you supposed to be straightforward when all human situations are by their nature full of contradictions and paradoxes? When you have to pursue several conflicting objectives simultaneously? How can you be predictable if you have to take decisions that ignore important factors and solid arguments, when you sense that at the same time you are also determining the repair bill that won't be due for another two years? The world can't be divided into either/or; it functions on the principle of "*both* this *and* that." Today it's like this, but perhaps tomorrow it will be different. Everything depends on circumstances. Managers are masters of paradox.

Under certain circumstances you will want to change your mind: people call that "learning." If trust hasn't been established, this can be interpreted as inconsistency and untrustworthiness. Could it be that learning is impeded by the need for credibility? And there is a further argument: I know quite a few managers whom nobody trusts even though they are absolutely straightforward and reliable; every member of staff can count on being fired if their performance is poor.

It is clear that consistent behaviour can help to *maintain* trust. But it isn't sufficient to *create* trust.

Admit mistakes

This is another requirement: you should sometimes show your weaknesses. Admit mistakes. Someone who plays the loser's game, covers up their own mistakes but exposes employees' mistakes cannot build trust. OK, that's fairly clear. But we also know that a lot of managers find it difficult to show their weaknesses as they have the means to conceal their mistakes. For a while at least. At the same time they openly admit that they are not perfect: "I am only human!" (the management version of confession). Simply saying "Of course I make mistakes!" is laughable and vain. It has no consequences for the manager. It is reasonably free of risk, unless you count the fact that it diminishes the manager's own ego. Admitting mistakes and revealing weakness – that is easy and trite when it comes from someone in the management hierarchy. But does it make a manager dependent on the employee? Does he take a serious risk in so doing? Probably not. Does he take a serious risk if he does not do so? Again, the answer is no. Let's think: what is important in the company? What is important is what has consequences. What is unimportant? What is unimportant is what has no consequences. Admitting mistakes has no consequences for a manger.

Be genuine

The famous Hollywood producer Samuel Goldwyn is said to have observed: "The secret of being a good actor is sincerity; if you can fake that, you've got it made."

No, managers shouldn't be actors, they shouldn't play any role. They should be genuine; they had best be authentic. Most people will probably agree with this statement. But it is too simplistic. What does "genuine" mean? Does it mean pinning your employees to the wall with the sheer force of your authenticity? Telling them exactly what you think without pulling any punches? Letting it all hang out? It's the tough guys in management who feel especially genuine. In power situations, the need for authenticity is material for a soap opera. Power *per se* tends to lead to a fall from grace when it comes to communication. A manager needs to remain aware of his role in the company and position in the hierarchy at all times – and that rules out genuineness. This applies especially in critical situations that staff experience as threatening.

At the very least, you shouldn't lie. That can be difficult; when the need for justification arises, telling lies can be the most natural thing. But let's talk about you. When someone forces you into a corner by asking "How could that happen?" or "Why didn't you watch out for that?," you'll present the situation in a way that makes you look as good as possible so that you get off scot-free. You'll emphasize one aspect and play down another. It's called lying. And it's clever. It helps people to survive. All lies are innocent lies. The Bible doesn't say "Thou shalt not lie"; it says "Thou shalt not bear false witness against thy neighbour." That's something different.

Mean what you say, and act accordingly

You mean what you say and act accordingly – and still no one trusts you. Have you ever found that? "Mean what you say" is too personal; it clings to your good intention in a rather feeble way. It ignores the effect of the system. If an employee refuses to trust you because you have different information and interests, and sees you (quite rightly) as an agent of capital, then clearly trust isn't developing very well. We are all dependent on the decision of the person we are dealing with, whether they consider us trustworthy or not. If they refuse to trust you or structural conditions prevent trust, there can be no trust-based interaction. It is impossible for trust to come about because one person wants it to; trust arises (or doesn't arise) when both parties confirm mutual trust. More about that later.

Nevertheless, if management declares in a quasi-religious tone that staff represent the company's most important resource or irreplaceable intangible assets, and then at the same time announces redundancies and cuts in the training budget, it should decide which it really means – its words or its actions – otherwise trust will never develop.

Keep your promises

Co-operation, keeping to agreements and trust often tend to be lumped together. We teach our children that promises must be kept. "You promised me that" means roughly the same as "You owe me." The imperative for successful co-operation is to keep your agreements. We tend to trust those who honour their arrangements – people who value results rather than endeavours, attempts and other stories of self-sacrifice. In some companies the only thing people keep to is the bookkeeping.

But what about you? Do you keep your promises? If you break your agreements (you may call it "adapting to different circumstances"), others will too. The newly appointed manager who has nothing better to do than keep hammering away at costs may say "Break all the contracts" when staff point out that agreements have been made with suppliers. How can I hope that a person will play by the company rules if I encourage him to break obligations to suppliers? It's people like this who prevent business being conducted in a sensible way. You yourself may think that an agreement is unimportant, but it may be central for someone else. Someone who doesn't keep his promises undermines himself. He'll have an inner sense that "I'm not capable of making agreements; I can't trust myself." He won't trust other people. So, when you've made an agreement, stick to it. Or else don't enter into agreements. You can always agree not to agree.

Of all the low-key forms of behaviour that are capable of maintaining trust, keeping promises seems to me the most attainable. It's a somewhat passive approach, but without it one can hardly begin the task of cultivating trust.

Borrow trust

The quality of goods can't always be assessed. Economics divides goods into three categories: *search goods* whose quality is known and which people simply have to find, such as potatoes; *experience goods* whose quality can be assessed only after use, such as new films; and *credence goods* whose quality can't be assessed by the ordinary consumer: which lawyer is the best? How safe is flying? Which surgeon does the best sutures? Which investment analyst recommends investments that will benefit me rather than him? Which company is worth working for? Which politician represents my interests? But sales people will also ask themselves the question "How can I get customers to trust me if they can't assess the quality of my product directly?" One answer is in a roundabout way, by bringing in a third party.

Left-wing politicians surround themselves with well-known business people to send the message: "You can trust me because of the companies I am looking after." New writers ask established authors for endorsements: favourable comments whose function is to transfer trust from the known to the unknown. A young person looking for his first job trusts a good friend's recommendation: "You can go there, that's a good company." We ask an expert whether he has experience with this or that appliance. We buy a magazine that evaluates consumer goods. We go to an independent doctor because someone wants to find out whether we are malingering or genuinely ill. Management brings consultants into the company so that they will give recommendations from an objective standpoint, although what they often do in practice is to present internal decisions from an external angle. Or people use the shop stewards' committee to settle a problem of conflicting procedures.

What connects all these examples? They describe a *triangle*. If someone doesn't trust or isn't sure whether he is regarded as trustworthy, he resorts to third parties from whom trust can, as it were, be borrowed. These third parties are expert systems that assess risk for us and give us information. Trust doesn't then run direct, but is channelled indirectly.

This is the mechanism: trustworthy institutions as third parties transfer reputation to something unknown. If the third parties who sell these assurance services verify your or your company's credibility by means of certificates, seals, tests, audits, licences or lists of ethical companies, the customer judges you accordingly. Some dealers can give you a trust seal that you can use to decorate your website. A huge industry of corrections improves and immunizes the object of organized original trust and gears it to that presumptuous old objective: banishing uncertainty and risk from human existence as far as possible.

The rationale is that customers need guidance in an increasingly complex world. But under the guise of trust and quality assurance, certificates are issued and refused, markets are protected and some easy ways of making a living are secured. Consider those archaic master craftsman's certificates or that ISO nonsense. Yes, people trust, but what they trust is not the market that ensures quality but the certificates that *claim* quality. Evidently, people trust the certificate-issuers more than their own suppliers. The fact that ISO and other third parties are flourishing is a sign of crisis. We have everything: we just don't have trust.

We tend to trust standards and regulations, but not people. Companies trust institutions more than their own staff. Systems, market protection mechanisms, over-regulated labour markets: everything has to be classified and subordinated. The free play of forces? Clear thinking? No chance! Christel Lane from the University of Cambridge investigated relationships between customers and suppliers in the German engineering industry, and concluded: "The high level of conformity to regulations leaves German managers little room for autonomous decisions and it hinders initiative. Technical standards for products are dictated by trade organizations. This does not give much incentive for innovations. The closed, narrow trust of German business relationships (based on specifications) means that German industry continues to produce small innovations and high quality. German companies are not well prepared to utilize the radical innovations of the future. The reason is that German industry has too much false trust." (Leadbeater, p. 165.)

And how problematic too much false trust can be becomes evident if we look at the American lawyer Robert Parker Junior. His system for grading wines has led to a situation where many wine drinkers will try only those wines that he has evaluated. They are seldom willing to experiment with anything new. Untested wines barely have a chance. Trust in Parker weakens wine enthusiasts' trust in their own taste.

Moving away from the idea of trust as a consolation prize

I don't want to dispute that all these aspects have an influence on the climate of trust. They do play a part in facilitating trust and improving the conditions for it, but they aren't powerful steps. Moreover, they are geared to a diminished form of trust. People make do with it because there is an almost unanimous opinion (in practice and in the literature) that there is no direct way to create trust. They say that trust is a by-product, an indirect result, a consequence that ensues from something else. According to this view, the manifestation of trust is passive. Consequently, trust remains mysterious, something you can't quite get at and certainly not something you can put into operation.

I'm now going to offer an active, direct way to make use of a powerful force. I'm going to treat trust as a core product to be brought about quickly, not a by-product to be cultivated slowly and indirectly. My suggestion is to put trust to the vote. After all, a discernible trust only arises when the *actions* of the person we are dealing with necessitate it. It is only through their actions that you can see whether someone is prepared to enter into a trusting relationship. But how can you get the other party to act?

At this point I'd like to re-emphasize that I'm proposing trust as a means of control. I'd like to clarify the little-understood economic mechanism behind the term. I want to be quite clear about the fact that my policy is to use trust to *influence behaviour*. This would only represent a moral problem if I were to conceal a manipulative intention.

To move from a negative to a positive definition and on to the practice of trust, I am proposing a way forward based on a theory of contracts. This may sound dry and academic, but in fact it is full of life, and I hope it will prove practicable for many people. Put simply, the perspective I have chosen is "You as manager." I'll talk about you as a trust-giver, and the employee as the trust-taker. So, what can you do to build trust? How do you start off the trust mechanism?

The implicit contract as a means of management

Business players interact. To achieve your aims, you have to enter into relationships with other players, relationships in which an exchange takes place. This exchange is based on more or less clear notions of a balance in giving and receiving. Your own interests may change during the process in a way that benefits both parties. As a rule, the parties involved don't know each other, or at least not well enough to justify trust on the basis of positive experience. That's why contracts are formed. Max Weber regarded contracts as the quintessence of modern industrialized society. Contracts are supposed to bring about security.

This also applies to relationships within a company in which performance is required and exchange takes place between manager and staff. People don't normally know each other before these relationships begin. It is no accident that a contract is made right at the beginning of the relationship: the employment contract. Some people think it advisable to supplement this contract later with additional contracts, such as target agreements. We could therefore describe management in terms of managing exchange-based relationships.

Contracts allow you to specify explicitly what is to be exchanged for what. They normally stipulate the compensation due if the partners fail to fulfil their obligations. That is the explicit contract.

However, the conduct of a partner can't be fully controlled. You can certainly influence it, but 100 percent certainty and predictability is out of the question. All contracts that we negotiate (employment contracts, target agreements, rental agreements, marriage contracts) are incomplete. There's always an element that isn't explicitly regulated, something unarticulated. A. Parsons calls this the non-contextual element of the contract. There is always room for discretion, which isn't explicitly regulated. Indeed, it can't be, otherwise our contracts would go into endless detail. This is why some civil codes include general clauses requiring people to act in good faith so as to cover all non-regulated matters.

So despite all the contracts and agreements, when you work with your staff you have to invest an element of faith: trust. No chain of command is so strong, no supervision so watertight, no contract so comprehensive that you can dispense with trust. You, the trusting party, expect the member of staff to use his discretion in a spirit of co-operation; at least you expect him not to act to your detriment. This management mechanism could be described as an implicit contract, in this case between you and the member of staff. Trust therefore strengthens uncertain expectations.

Let us complete the picture: the member of staff also naturally has an implicit contract with you as a representative of the organization. This implicit contract, often referred to as a psychological contract, is actually a bundle of mutual expectations for which there is no written assurance. For example, the organization offers promotion prospects, outstanding opportunities for learning, prestige, a pleasant atmosphere and fair treatment. In return, the member of staff provides commitment, innovation, flexibility, willingness to learn, loyalty and perhaps even a high level of sacrifice of his personal life. From the employee's point of view, the calculation could be something like this: "If I work really hard here and complete the project successfully, I will soon be promoted." He calculates probability, but he can never be certain that his expectations will be met.

The content of the implicit contract may change. It depends on changes in society. If the current generation of employees regard their jobs as short-term arrangements rather than lifelong agreements, they will expect their companies to give them something short-term, flexible and transferable in return. If a company aspires to be an employer of choice, it will do well to take note of changing patterns of employment in society to ensure that it isn't offering something that nobody wants. Overlook this and you will have trouble recruiting and retaining good people. M. Dickmann reports on a study in a large clinic where the management interpreted the implicit contract as an expectation of constant salary increases. What the staff really wanted was to be able to arrange their own duty rosters and manage their own working time; in fact, money ranked seventh in their list of priorities.

A trusting relationship is characterized by the expectation that the dependency involved in the relationship will not be exploited by one of the parties. Once again: this contract is only implicit (or psychological) insofar as it hasn't been specified verbally or in writing. The implicit contract *is* trust.

So we always have an explicit and an implicit contract. On the basis of the explicit contract, we can take legal action in respect of a duty of care. The implicit contract goes further: it relates to responsibility. It's impossible to generalize about the relative sizes of the two. Banks normally have a lot of regulation; this means a large explicit contract. Advertising agencies and partnerships have a wide trust margin; this means a large implicit contract. Within an employment relationship, the exchange relationship in the explicit contract is "money for work." In the implicit contract, it is "security for loyalty." It isn't hard to see that in many companies the balance has shifted to the explicit contract.

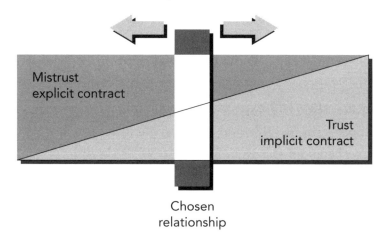

Mistrust
explicit contract

Trust
implicit contract

Chosen
relationship

If we take a closer look, the content of the implicit contract consists of three elements:

- the employee performs what the manager expects or what has been agreed
- the manager refrains from explicit checking and control mechanisms
- each party conducts itself in the spirit of the explicit contract.

If, for example, an employee wants to show that he is worthy of the trust placed in him, he must invest his energy. He has to exert himself. He will do that as long as the realizable benefit exceeds the cost of his behaviour. Just cold calculation? (According to Goethe.) Soulless? (According to Schlegel.) It might sound that way. There are many possible types of benefit: money, prestige, job security, character-building activity, social contact, recognition, perhaps even self-respect (the sense of being fair, acting with commitment, doing something that gives pleasure, fulfilling a sense of honour). It can be highly advantageous for people to confirm trust if they value the space to be themselves, manage themselves and be respected. And the benefits are greater if they coincide with the maximum benefit for the manager: if both are pursuing interests in the same direction.

Starting trust

How can you know that the other person will keep to the rules of the agreement and the spirit of co-operation? If you can't be sure, why should you stick to the agreement? If you opt for trust, you have to go through the firewall of doubt without knowing whether what you find on the other side will make the investment worth while. Courts, lawyers, moralists and the rest of us are constantly dealing with breaches of trust. So once again, who is going to guarantee that your employee won't cheat on you?

No one. Your expectations as a giver of trust may remain unfulfilled. The trust you invest in advance may be abused at any time. The employee you trust can decide whether he is going to honour that trust or disappoint you. He has an advantage over you insofar as he knows what he is willing to do. And he knows his own ability. He has intimate information about himself, his calculation of benefit and his secret objectives. He knows whether he is trustworthy, whether he is capable of entering into agreements.

If you nevertheless trust, you consciously choose uncertainty, loss of control and the possibility of disappointment. You give the employee a task without knowing whether he will prove worthy of your trust; you don't know whether he will use his freedom of action to your detriment. So placing trust initially involves *risk* for you as a manager. This risky advance investment can't be justified in an absolute sense, but it is extremely reasonable, as we shall see.

So how do you start the trust mechanism, if that's what you want to do? If you're going to choose the direct way, the fast, active way, then there is only one answer:

Vulnerability starts trust.

You get the trust mechanism going by actively making yourself vulnerable. Vulnerability is the instrument with which you begin the trust relationship. It's your investment that you have to worry about if there is a possibility of trust. And the greater the damage you could incur, the greater your investment of trust.

Please note: you actively make yourself vulnerable. You do that by extending the implicit contract at the expense of the explicit. You dispense with overt security measures, abolish rules, dismantle the control system, loosen access restrictions, abandon additional reporting. It doesn't have to be either/or; you can increase the employee's scope for discretion and alter the type and quantity of tasks you entrust. I'll give some examples later. The

98

important thing is that the risks you take will be watched carefully by others. They are signals of trust.

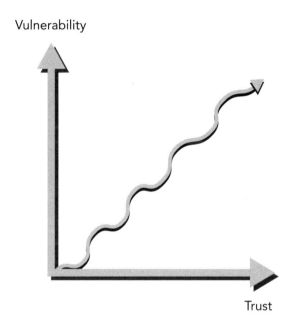

Active trust, then, is accepted vulnerability. If you want to build trust, you actively grant someone the opportunity to act injuriously, while being confident that they won't take up that opportunity. You say to yourself "I don't rule out the possibility that they could exploit my trust, but I consider it unlikely." Trust is a bet on the gain achieved by trust that also entails the risk of loss.

The connection between vulnerability and trust was described vividly by the actor Joseph Fiennes in an interview when he was asked about nude scenes: "You are conscious that you are naked, and everyone else is dressed. It's a slightly unnatural setting. But the fear is not physical exposure; it's the way it's going to be shot, edited and perceived. So really it's about trusting a good director." (*InStyle*, September 2001, p. 268.)

But what we have said so far doesn't explain why vulnerability determines trust. Why is it that you set off the trust mechanism with vulnerability?

The binding power of trust

A man bought more than he expected when he went to a market in Berlin. As he was leaving, he noticed a valuable book on a second-hand bookstall. He said to his wife, "What a pity. I'd like to buy that book, but we've spent all our money." The woman behind the counter said, "Take the book; you can transfer the money to my bank account." "But I come from another city," he replied, surprised. "We don't know each other. What makes you so sure I will transfer the money? Don't you even want to take my name?" She didn't. The man had to smile to himself as he went to work a little late on Monday morning; he'd been to the bank when it opened at 8.30, wanting to be the first person to fill in a transfer slip.

That's how the story was told to me. It shows the great effect of trust, something that neither power nor money can come close to: trust brings *commitment*. It creates obligation. It binds. It unleashes a deep current from which we can barely escape. And the greater the risky advance investment, the greater the binding effect. People have done incredible things because others trusted them. Why? What psychological mechanisms are at work?

As human beings, we look for balance. Give and take need to balance if we are to experience a sense of ease. Such is the law of reciprocity. It calls out to us "If someone gives you a gift, give *them* a gift to make things even." When we get something, be it nice or valuable, we lose our independence for a moment. The other person has invested something in us. This puts our relationship out of kilter. We feel a sense of obligation to them. If we are considered trustworthy, we feel a pressure we can alleviate only by giving something back. In our case, this means acting in a manner worthy of the trust we have been shown. The effect of being trusted is like a mortgage. "As with a gift, it is also possible to bind someone by showing trust." (Niklas Luhmann) On an everyday level, we've all experienced the binding effect of trust: the boss pats the up-and-coming youngster on the shoulder, looks deep into his eyes and says with great conviction, "I'm counting on you." Who could escape the force of this gesture?

We all know the feeling, an almost astonished sense of being honoured, when someone unexpectedly shows us trust. We feel disarmed. Everyone knows the most powerful example from crime thrillers: the policeman who puts his gun away in order to talk to the criminal. Psychopaths apart, everyone has conscience, self-respect and a sense of shame, and they yield to them. In 1580, Montaigne described the mechanism thus: "The person I trust with the money when we travel, I trust him completely. I don't check at all. He could easily cheat when the books are added up. And if he is not the devil, I force him to be honest by being so totally trusting."

But isn't that moral? No, it's *amoral*. It isn't saying "You should." It's a calculation that takes account of the feeling of balance and reciprocity that people carry within them. This trust almost has an element of compulsion. Some people may associate it with the idea of a good life. But actually it doesn't matter; in the end, it makes no difference what your motives for being trustworthy are. Whether you behave in a trustworthy manner through moral obligation because you believe in fairness, or because it's in your interest to be seen as credible makes no difference to the end result. The difference is in the sympathy value, not the outcome. Weak trust is quite adequate for that.

The important thing is that giving trust is a gift that creates obligations *precisely because it is difficult or impossible to demand.* It's like paying in money to an imaginary relationship account so that compensation is due from the other person if they are to avoid an inner sense of discomfort. Consequently, trust is often justified after the event even if circumstances initially made it appear unjustified. People frequently reject trust categorically in order to *avoid* the binding effect; after all, our willingness and capacity for trust are limited. Sometimes people don't want to be trusted at all if they are aware of their own unreliability and like the other person. When they say things like "I don't deserve your trust" or "It's better not to trust me too much," they reveal that they as recipients of trust are afraid of the associated obligation. They anticipate the shame they will feel if they are unable to justify the trust placed in them.

Similarly, employees often want to avoid the sense of obligation associated with trust, preferring exchange relationships based on quantities and systems: three sacks of overtime for three sacks of money. Since they don't trust their manager or their colleagues ("Who's not working enough here?") they tend to want payment to relate to their presence rather than their completion of tasks. They often reject trust-based working time because they are afraid of the associated obligation. In my experience, the introduction of trust-based working time fails not so much because of mistrustful management or employees' concerns about justification, but because of the power that comes from trust.

Our considerations have reached a point where the problem of control addressed earlier can be shown in a new light. It has now become clear that two things that appeared mutually exclusive actually belong together: trust and control. Trust controls the behaviour of another person. It is wrong to play trust and control off against each other. The opposite applies:

Trust is control.

The binding effect of trust is an anthropological constant. There is no aspect of culture in which this phenomenon is unknown. In some cultures, it is the basis of social life. As Hotspur said to Henry IV: "But I tell you, my lord fool, out of this nettle, danger, we pluck this flower, safety."

How you make yourself vulnerable

When Andrew Grove and Gordon Moore founded Intel, they had neither a product nor a business plan. Afterwards, Grove reflected that the fact that the venture capital company provided the finance out of trust in him had a stronger binding effect than any contract could have done.

There are several examples of an almost total lack of explicit contracts. Consider the handshake with which McDonald's and Coca-Cola renew their co-operation each year, a trust relationship that has been operating since 1954. Elvis Presley had no written contract with his manager Colonel Tom Parker, yet their co-operation lasted until Elvis's death. There are no acceptance contracts between the cosmetic group Laboratoire Biosthétique and its customers, and one price applies to everyone, so nobody needs to feel that they negotiated badly. Customers can give notice of termination for the end of the month without giving reasons. Star Alliance bases its co-operation on a contract running to just four pages, a trust arrangement that evidently works; in any case, a combined effort succeeded in seeing off a hostile takeover bid for Alliance partner Air Canada. "A balance of power that requires the management to be able to share power because they trust," according to Lufthansa executive board member Thomas Sattelberger.

Comparable arrangements can be found in the world of high technology in the form of co-destiny and the integration of suppliers. The purchaser shows trust in the seller by means of exclusive supply rights. In this way, the supplier makes itself highly dependent on the customer. It seems paradoxical, but it is the partners' ability to switch that creates the conditions for potential long-term relationships. As we have seen, trust binds. Freedom creates obligation. The strength of networks and loose associations is what Mark Granovetter calls "weak ties."

If we now look at what you do as a manager, you have choices. You make yourself vulnerable, for example:

- if your employee finds it difficult to leave the company because he senses that you are relying on him, that he is really needed
- if you have given your employee a truly important task and you don't constantly look over his shoulder but instead trust him to come to you if he needs to check or discuss something
- if you don't seize control of difficult situations and claim them as matters for management, giving the employee responsibility instead
- if you don't keep your important market and customer contacts to yourself, but trust your staff with them (which means taking a risk with your own value)
- if you pass on information to your staff that could cause you damage if it were misused

- if it is manifestly the case that "Without you, I'd be up the creek without a paddle."

If you as a manager place your fate in the hands of your staff, if you relinquish your power and ability to act arbitrarily, if you allow staff to take responsibility for things that will affect your success, then the binding effect of trust can develop. Are your staff aware that you will be damaged if they don't do their job? It isn't enough to say "I need your contribution"; your staff must be aware that you'll have a problem if they don't do their job. If a member of staff is justified in feeling that their contribution hardly counts, has little effect and isn't indispensable, no trust can develop.

I'd like to illustrate this with the example of a tough manager keen on restructuring. During times of change management, which he has successfully dealt with again and again, his staff will have been well advised to distrust him. It doesn't take a genius to see that a company that destroys value has no economic right to exist. Now, a few years later, when the company can be built up again, he lets his staff know, in a slightly indirect way, "If you don't achieve the required return on equity, we'll get rid of you." Instead of linking his fate to that of his staff, instead of showing them that they matter, instead of trusting them, he is using the old method of creating fear. This is a mistake. The company hasn't been making any headway for years.

Here's another example of what not to do. The finance director of a holding company starts a PowerPoint presentation. On the screen you see a colourful array of bars and figures. He explains to the group of managers that these are the results of discussions on targets; they have been agreed with the executive boards of the individual companies. He then points to a shaded area in the upper part of the chart, and identifies it as the safety reserve, a provision built in in case the targets aren't achieved. So what is the first message? "I don't trust you." What is the second message? "Agreements aren't agreements." What is the third message? "None of this is to be taken seriously." The executive board of the holding company hasn't allowed itself to be vulnerable. It doesn't trust its staff's performance. And yet it is surprised when targets aren't met year after year.

Let's go back to vulnerability.

- Trust people to have their own quality standards for themselves and their work. Agree on results, and then let each person find their own way to achieve them. Everyone can achieve results in a way that suits them. If you trust, it's only the results that count.

- Get rid of time-monitoring systems. No one can seriously claim that an eight-hour day in the office will stimulate innovative ideas. And it's no good deciding that people need to do their work in a set time; they need to manage their own time in a way that best meets the needs of internal and external customers. Working with responsibility for results requires people to take responsibility for their own work and time management. Those who can't do it can learn.

- Take customer orientation seriously. Support unorthodox decisions made by your staff. Mitchell Kertzman, CEO at Sybase, put it like this: "Suppose I have an employee who visits a customer late in the evening. To solve the customer's problem, the employee has to give him a promise that will actually cost money. It's in all our interests that he should do the right thing for the customer.... He does not need to expect a telling-off even if the promise he made to the customer is not standard procedure. If it helped to the customer in this particular case, then the employee did the right thing."

- Check first, then trust. If you have selected a new member of staff, you'll soon find out that he doesn't fully come up to your expectations. He is just different from you: his habits, ways of thinking and priorities won't be the same as yours. This is a breeding-ground for misunderstandings, disputes and doubts. "Did I make a mistake there? Is he really the right person?" No, you should trust yourself. You considered all the options, and then you made a decision. Now stand by it.
- Put yourself to the test with your staff: give them the opportunity to vote you out. This is the highest level of vulnerability possible at work. It's the ultimate level of trust.

Trust becomes possible when you make yourself dependent on the agreement and performance of your staff.

Trust is facilitated when each party allows the other to vote for or against them. If the human resources department sense they are encountering distrust, they can do something about it: they can make themselves vulnerable. How? By not imposing their plan, but putting it to the vote. If they are convinced of the value of what they have to offer, they will let their internal customers decide whether or not they want it. But if they don't trust line managers' judgement and impose their plan on them, they will find trust is withdrawn. And rightly so.

On Western Digital's website, questions relating to technical problems are answered by technical customer service staff in a very short time (over 90 percent within an hour). Where does trust come in? All the Q&A correspondence is freely accessible, so that customers may be able to resolve their queries by looking at previous dialogues. Customers know that products don't always work perfectly; all sorts of problems and difficulties can arise. But this website gives customers the impression that the company isn't trying to conceal the truth. It is making itself vulnerable. It even gives me active reasons not to opt for it.

Trust binds – and the effect is similar to that of responsibility. A term such as faith or confidence could constitute a bridge between the two. Where responsibility is accepted and fulfilled, you get reliable sequences of actions. Then you can be sure that the patient will receive the right medical attention, the night nurse will check their temperature and you will be contacted if there is an emergency. Responsibility has the effect of a guarantee – not of success, but that an action will be carried out with care.

I experienced an interesting incident that illustrates this point. I was called in to see a large car manufacturer whose rate of absence had been increasing steadily for years. There was a dramatic difference between two plants at the same company: in plant A the rate of absence was 8 percent, whereas in plant B it was only 4 percent. Management started taking countermeasures. They decided on campaigns and initiatives to reduce the absence rate at plant A. What happened? It increased! It rose by an average of half a percent per year. Why? Management ignored the simple fact that people had reasons for staying at home. The pressure to change produced resistance. The situation in sick organizations is: "If you didn't apply pressure like this, I wouldn't have to push in the other direction." But what reasons could there have been?

What was noticeable was that plant B organized work around teams, yet each individual team member carried out a special task. Team-based work also existed in plant A, but unlike plant B, it emphasized the idea that every team member needed to be able to do the job of every other member if necessary. Something that might be experienced as job enrichment in a trust-based context (and was intended as such here) was perceived quite differently: staff presumed that management didn't trust their commitment, and so took safety measures and made emergency provisions. A climate of distrust prevailed. The hidden message was: "We don't believe we can rely on you. That's why we are spreading responsibilities across a large number of people." The consequence of this form of work organization was that staff felt dispensable: "If I don't do it, someone else will." Someone who is dispensable doesn't experience the binding effect of "It all depends on me." He doesn't experience the trust invested in him by the company. In plant B, by contrast, management had confidence in the workers and believed they could trust most of them, even to the point of risking damage. Management allowed vulnerability, and were rewarded by a lower absence rate. That was the trust dividend.

To be sure, the work organization in plant A could be seen as positive: an honest attempt to free up routines and enrich tasks. But it does have a downside: popularity and replaceability. Which is to be preferred? No extremes work. And which side people experience most intensively depends on the context, the climate and the trust/mistrust ratio. If trust predominates, checking has an informative, supportive role. If distrust predominates, checking is experienced as restrictive and inimical to trust.

E-business provides an example of trust as an effective approach in business. The growth of eBay, the most successful internet company in the world, is based on two factors: the worldwide proliferation of the internet and confidence in its trust mechanism. Its customer list has 35 million names – buyers and sellers from all over the world – and yet hardly anyone knows the party they are dealing with. People operate on the assumption that someone on the other side of the world will actually transfer the money or send the goods. "We have an annual turnover in excess of $10 billion based exclusively on trust," says CEO Rajiv Dutta, "because we believe that people are fundamentally trustworthy." The trust is repaid in the overwhelming majority of cases. Participants find each other on line and benefit from a convenient way to buy and sell. They exchange a few words and often develop friendships across the world. Dutta says the exceptions are so few they're not worth mentioning.

To give trust, then, only *appears* unreasonable or irrational. Like water, it is a strong thing that endures because it seems to be weak. The weaker ties are the stronger ones. So it isn't the explicit contract but the implicit one, the unarticulated one, that is the decisive factor. In his bequest setting up the foundation that bears his name, Robert Bosch wrote: "The letter kills, but the spirit gives life."

What we let go of remains.

For my final illustration, I'd like to use a telephone conversation with a manager who asked me for advice. I'll quote it from memory:

"I have a member of staff who I think is highly motivated, but I have doubts about his ability. He just doesn't have the experience needed for this project. But I trust him all the same."

"Only in a limited way. You trust his willingness to work, but not his capability. If a wealth of experience is critical for success in this job, then you've chosen the wrong person."

"That may be, but he was the only one available. That's the way it is. But I've agreed with him that he's to give me a brief overview of the project's progress every Monday. That seems a reasonable solution to me."

"Yes, that's a reasonable solution, but it follows the reason of distrust. If you choose the reason of trust instead, you will do without the weekly report. Show him a sign of trust: agree that he needs to come to you on his own initiative when questions arise or if he is in doubt about a decision. That doesn't solve the problem of the wrong person doing the job, but it keeps the relationship on a trust footing."

"What if he doesn't see a problem that's coming up?"

"Well yes, if he isn't in a position to identify questions when they arise, it would be better for you to take over the job yourself. But do you think you yourself always see problems coming? It sounds a bit as though you alone have prudence and foresight, and your member of staff is like a dependent child. In both cases I would advise you to terminate the co-operation."

"That's easy for you to say. Should I just stand by and watch him fall into a trap?"

"You can make that decision in each individual case. It may be that the trap isn't there any more, even if it was before. And if he does make a mistake, and it costs money, and the worst comes to the worst, you can count it as an investment in his training."

"It isn't very nice to invest six-figure sums in the training of one member of staff."

"No, certainly not. But neither is it very nice to be excessively cautious and then exploit his cultivated helplessness in order to feel indispensable."

No one can ask for trust in a credible way without having allowed themselves to be vulnerable.

Active truthfulness

As we have demonstrated, you get the trust mechanism started when you *yourself* give trust *first* by allowing yourself to be vulnerable. This is the most important condition. You are vulnerable when an abuse of trust by the other person would be hugely detrimental to you. If we look at the subject of *communication*, you are vulnerable when you open yourself up, when you are truthful, when harm can be done. On the listener's side, this means mostly remaining silent, although one can ask questions to clarify content. It involves a willingness to understand. It doesn't mean considering one's own response while the other person is still speaking. Above all, it doesn't mean justifying or defending oneself. It's better to say clearly "Thank you for your openness."

On the speaker's side, this means communicating one's own perception honestly and directly and without embellishment. It means not putting off saying something. It means not claiming to have the truth, but expressing one's perception just as it is. In a nutshell, it means being genuinely truthful. But it means especially not keeping quiet about anything. After all, you are responsible not just for what you do but for what you *don't* do. This is something most people don't want to take responsibility for.

Now, truthfulness is important to many people. It is seen as a fundamental requirement in a trusting relationship. However, what people normally mean by this could be summed up as "Thou shalt not lie." That in turn means not wilfully manipulating information to one's own advantage or deliberately misrepresenting facts. It means answering questions to the best of one's knowledge and belief. Nevertheless, this is merely the *passive* side of truthfulness. Merely refraining from telling lies doesn't make one vulnerable.

But what if you aren't asked? If you aren't expressly called up to give an answer? There is also the lie that can be effectively told by silence. You also lie if you have the sense that you ought to communicate something to someone because he will otherwise believe that everything is OK. Or because he will otherwise proceed on the basis of incorrect assumptions. Or if the statement you could make would help the other person. Or if the other person would be disadvantaged by your silence.

So there is also an *active* truthfulness that takes the initiative to speak without being expressly asked; it takes a stand without being called upon to do so. You do this simply because you think it is important between you and the other person. Active truthfulness takes responsibility. The Judaeo-Christian idea of truth includes the concept of sincerity: the absence of deceitful intention or ambiguity in personal relationships. The Hebrew word for truth, *Ehmet*, also means trust. The other person knows he can rely on you: you won't let him walk right into a trap. If you think something is important for your co-operation, you will address it without having to be asked. The rest may hide behind noble manners.

Active truthfulness supports trust.

Wesley Clark, commander-in-chief of Nato troops in the Balkans, reports something a colleague, officer Peter Pace, said to him. When Clark wanted US marines in the Balkans, Pace thought it was a bad idea, and told him: "If you want them, they're yours. But when the Pentagon asks what I think, I'll oppose your plan for the following reasons...." Clark comments: "I was confident that Pace would speak truth to any authority. I could really trust him.

Leaders don't have confidence in yes-men." (*Fast Company*, 11, 2001, p. 72.)

No one wants to be responsible for silence. That's why people look for relief. One way of securing it is to take the moral high ground. People identify problems externally; they accuse others: "He's always so vindictive!" "She takes offence so easily!" Behind the accusation is cowardice. Another way is to portray your silence dishonestly, presenting it as something positive: "I must spare their feelings." I have said it before and I say it again: protecting someone in this way means depriving them of the ability to make decisions. You place yourself above that person, you decide what is and isn't reasonable for them to accept. You abandon the domain of equality and responsibility. You push the other person into the role of a child. It offends human dignity when you take away someone's ability to take responsibility or curtail it in a disempowering way.

But it's more complicated than that. What you really want is not so much to protect the other person; you want to protect *yourself*. Because you fear loss of love. Because you don't want to reveal weakness. Because you don't want to be vulnerable. Because you fear: "They won't like me any more if I'm honest." "It might degenerate into a quarrel." "He might get me back some other way."

Of course, no one likes to be the bearer of bad news. But many managers are so afraid of it that they become passive. What they overlook is the power that can develop from what isn't said. It may take a different form in order to be expressed: bottled-up anger; an increasingly negative distorted view of the other person, which soon becomes the basis for interpreting every form of behaviour; malicious comments behind your back; a powerful alliance of your whole department against you; the complaint made by a member of your staff direct to your boss... Don't make the mistake of thinking your employee is stupid. He will have picked up what you haven't said long ago. You can't be that good at pretending. A feeling of uneasiness about another person communicates itself in many ways other than language.

If you don't address problems openly with your member of staff, the response will be opposition, defensiveness, withdrawal or attack. You can get the same reaction in a discussion – but the inestimable advantage is that both parties put their cards on the table and you spare yourself a lot of painful roundabout ways of getting to the root of the problem.

However, when you have decided to put active truthfulness at the centre of your communication, you have taken only the first step. We shrink from truthfulness because it is a powerful force that can unleash strong reactions, both positive and negative. Anyone who invokes such a force should first pay serious attention to the issue of how to deal with it responsibly. In particular, discussions involving criticism or conflict, and especially appraisal interviews, need to be conducted in such a way that you solve problems instead of creating new ones. You can hardly engage in such discussions when you are standing in the doorway.

Does trust look forward or backward?

So is trust a prerequisite for successful co-operation or the consequence of it? Does it look forwards or backwards? The experts have a tough time with this question. The old reasoning stressed the result: the trust that materializes. Modern thinking stresses the prerequisite: the trust that you decide on. Let's take a look at this question in the light of our current understanding.

When you trust someone, you engender a strong feeling of responsibility on their part. You encourage a feeling of commitment.

Trusting other people encourages them to trust us. So trust brings about the very behaviour that from a logical point of view appears to be the prerequisite for trust. The risk you take allows you to start the upward spiral of trust. Seneca wrote: "Regard him as loyal, and you will make him loyal."

When human beings are treated as responsible people, they behave as such. We know from research that we are strongly influenced by other people's opinion of us. The other person is, or can become, a person of integrity if we give them the opportunity to confirm trust.

The opposite also applies. If you mistrust other people, they behave accordingly. If your employee is honest but you mistrust him for whatever reason, you are inviting him to accept the dishonest role. And the invitation to distrust is so powerful that hardly anyone can resist it. If, on the other hand, you distrust someone who really *is* dishonest, you merely reinforce his dishonesty. That has a dramatic consequence: *if you distrust, you never have the chance to encounter a trustworthy person*. With your mistrust, you bring about the very situation you fear. And you then manage that situation. You actively shape what you think you are just passively perceiving and reacting to. When you push what you think will save you to the fore, you increase the danger. You increase it by your very action. In this way you never manage to break the vicious circle of mistrust.

We may be encouraged by a well-known finding from the sphere of therapy. You give a person a valuable object. You say you are counting on that person and putting responsibility for your well-being in their hands. They are surprised and moved, and feel compelled to confirm your expectation. Now comes the interesting part. Even when someone who has proved himself dishonest is trusted, the trust is often confirmed. The explanation is that the moral imbalance between the trusting person and the other person's dishonesty is experienced in a way that provides a motive to compensate for the difference. Studies of the self-fulfilling prophecy clearly show that people who are treated as trustworthy tend to behave accordingly. In any case, the message "I trust you" is more effective in bringing about a desired outcome than "Trust me." It invests something before it expects anything; it gives first and then receives.

Of course there are limits: such trust would be inappropriate in some contexts. The risks, especially for third parties, would simply be too great. A probation officer who told a serial offender "Now I trust you, behave yourself and I'll expect you back on Sunday at 9 p.m." would be guilty of inexcusable negligence.

Nevertheless, the fact remains that trust is neither a prerequisite nor a result. It is *both*. It oscillates between prerequisite and confirmation. Trust runs in a *circular* pattern. So does mistrust.

The first step

But who should take the first step? This question has almost answered itself. All the same, I'd like to make a few brief comments against the background of the practical difficulties that may be encountered.

Controlling behaviour is especially prevalent in situations with uneven power relationships: employer and employee, parent and child, teacher and pupil, trainer and player. Consequently, people usually say that trust is something initiated by the stronger party: the person who can afford to make himself vulnerable. This stronger party is traditionally identified as the manager; the role of the weaker person is ascribed to the staff member. It is said that management must take the initiative. Is this basic assumption still valid in all cases? I believe it is no longer tenable. The stronger party is no longer necessarily the manager. At a time when growth in many companies is limited by qualitative and frequently also quantitative bottlenecks in the labour market, we need to revise our perspective. In any case the roles are no longer so clear: the person who gives work is not automatically the one who gives trust, and the person who receives work is not necessarily the one who receives trust. When partners have equal power and autonomy, attempts at control fail.

This shift in roles also makes it more likely that each player will be both a giver and receiver of trust in relation to the other party. A high level of trust results from an increasing vulnerability *on both sides*. Trust is therefore not a *by-product* of a good relationship, but the main *engine* that drives it. So there is a mutual relationship based on trust and contract whereby both managers and staff assume the position of trust-giver in relation to particular *expectations* and the position of trust-receiver with regard to particular *obligations*. And the way a role is organized is also decisive. For example, as a manager actively validated by staff one tends to be a receiver of trust; as a superior merely appointed by the hierarchy one tends to be a giver of trust. The difference emerges clearly in practice: you see it in the results.

Relationships necessarily consist of at least two parties, but it often only takes one to change the quality. So who should start? The manager can do this in a hierarchical organization. But it doesn't have to be the manager. Staff can do it too. However, if you always wait for the other person, you are letting go of the steering-wheel in your life. If no one is willing to go first, nothing will change. Then it's up to you to take the first step. You don't have control of the other person, but you have control of yourself. Take that step! Wherever you are in the hierarchy, there is only one way:

Here is the paradox: weakness is strength. The only way to create trust directly is through vulnerability. It is only when you allow yourself to be vulnerable that the binding effect of trust develops. It is only when you grant the other person the opportunity to do you serious harm that the economically significant management mechanism of trust develops. It is only when you are prepared to relinquish power and regard management as a service that you are on the right path.

These are, of course, uncomfortable conclusions for managers who normally do everything to bring about the opposite: they try to create invulnerability and power while imposing high costs of vulnerability on others by denying trust and hurting people with their mistrust. It is *because* so many managers fear vulnerability more than anything else that there is so little trust in companies.

This dominant (in both senses) management concept represents a massive hindrance to the development of trust. After all, managers are normally required to regulate things, to have things under control and to prevent vulnerability. In bookshops you can find titles like *How to Become Invulnerable*. In this way, everything is created except trust.

Management must not expect trust. It works like a boomerang: you have to initiate trust yourself, then it comes back. It's a one-way sequence. You can't demand trust; if you do, it shows that something has failed. We get much more when we trust. The great Scottish writer George MacDonald said: "To be trusted is a greater compliment than to be loved."

119

How you destroy trust

When someone no longer wants to rely on others, they demand security first, more security second, and finally they demand guarantees for this security. Trust is shaken. The residual risk that you can't control and are therefore forced to accept – the personal and historical disappointments, the extremely legalistic nature of the conditions in which we live, the intensification of hierarchical responsibility in companies that involves providing justification for things that have happened, the tendency to go to court for anything and everything, pursuing resource and compensation claims for millions, the foul blend of political correctness and self-victimization in society – all this creates a need in many people for protection and security. Everywhere we see an excessive concern with security that comes from a philosophy expressed as a capacity for absolute justification. Just as the behaviour of employers and unions in society takes place within a narrow framework of guarantee, liability and legal enforcement, so there is an escalation in the interplay between loss of trust and the demand for security in companies.

The sad mentality of caution: it is in hierarchies where the emphasis has shifted dramatically from responsibility for *tasks* to responsibility in terms of *accountability* that there is constant dissatisfaction with conditions in the company. Everywhere, the question "Where were you when that happened?" creates the mixture of uncertainty and fear that turns trust into a constraint. Trust is sacrificed when people decide to take a safety measure to deal with a risk that may initially have been small. On the level of control and safety that is then reached, every accident, every failure and every breakdown becomes an occasion for increased safety requirements. New standards, limits and technical regulations are introduced. *Every new rule creates more requirements for regulation.* Trust diminishes even more. A vicious circle begins. This is how it was with Mr Peters and Mrs Winter.

Mr Peters and Mrs Winter worked in the same company. They had known each other for years. Mr Peters already had a negative impression of Mrs Winter before he joined the company. A distant acquaintance, who had also worked at the company had told him that Mrs Winter had been suspected of embezzlement at a previous company, although it had never been proved. When he met her for the first time, she seemed nervous and agitated and unable to look him in the eye. Mr Peters felt his impression was confirmed. Although he tried to resist it and didn't want to be taken in by hearsay, the unpleasant feeling remained. He couldn't help suspecting that something wasn't right with Mrs Winter. Consequently, he gave her only the absolutely essential information, even when they worked closely together on projects. When he was her manager from time to time, he restricted her room for manoeuvre. He excluded her from circles in which information was shared and he increased the frequency of reporting. It was clear to Mrs Winter that Mr Peters did not trust her. She didn't know why. She had always been competent and reliable, and she found Mr Peters' behaviour inexplicable and clouded with prejudice. She became increasingly irritated. She suspected that Mr Peters bore her some personal ill will, and spoke privately of harassment.

If we think in terms of an individual case, why should I *not* trust someone if it has been established that they have lied to another person? Do I have precise information about the circumstances? What would the truth have been in this case? To what extent had the person who was deceived induced the lie by pressure for justification? If a person breaks contracts with other people in order to help me, why should I not trust them (in relation to me)?

But as mistrust has the tendency to be confirmed in human relationships, that spiral of mistrust begins and now characterizes the internal nature of companies. I will now ask the reader to pay very careful attention. We are coming to the core of my argument.

The process goes like this: if you become distrustful for any reason, you will introduce what you might refer to among your colleagues as tighter management. You tighten up observation, control and checking. Internal reporting, monitoring and other safety measures are intensified. Rules are introduced to distinguish what is allowed from what is forbidden. Working time is recorded. Agreements on objectives are defined more stringently. It's not just results that are agreed but also the way to achieve them. Staff experience this as a withdrawal of trust: a *breach of the implicit contract*.

The member of staff no longer senses goodwill on your part. People complain about low esteem, especially in relation to senior staff, and about the cold-blooded way people are dealt with in the department. If people sense they can't expect management to act with consistency and goodwill, there will be a disintegration of the trust that has been built up, in the sense of both cognitive and emotional security. And since one's relationship with one's employer is the basis of one's identity at work, this mistrust has an undermining effect at an existential level. Social reality ceases to be stable and reliable. The sense of security people have in dealing with one another is lost. People have to be on their guard. Employees will automatically interpret a manager's actions as detrimental to them.

Although (or precisely because) this breach of trust is frequently *felt* more than penetrated analytically, the consequences are concrete and far-reaching. The member of staff feels less dutybound to the manager, less committed. They reduce their efforts to justify the trust placed in them. Their inner motivation dwindles. Because they are controlled and regarded with distrust, they feel positively encouraged to be uncooperative; the inner psychological cost of a bad conscience no longer applies.

I say it again because it is important to me: when you withdraw trust from an employee, they don't have to balance the relationship account by contributing something in return. They no longer experience an inner pressure pushing them to restore the balance. They no longer have a bad conscience about cheating on you because you don't consider them trustworthy anyway. "You mistrust me, I cheat on you." Or: "You needn't worry if you've no reputation to lose." Seneca wrote 2000 years ago: "By your suspicion you have given the other person the right to sin against you."

After the first (frequently quiet) utterances of annoyance, the employee changes their behaviour. They make less effort, don't take any more risk, and withhold information. Their work ethic declines further, which in turn appears to justify your mistrust. You think you have been proved right: "I knew it!" You react to the deterioration in the work results and try to compensate for the loss of motivation with additional management measures. You intensify control. That costs time and money; the effect is mediocre. After all, the intensified monitoring system works only until ways are found of getting around it again. We know that control merely stimulates those who are controlled to be creative in rendering the control as ineffective as possible. Every regulation creates new system circumvention intelligence; innovative control mechanisms bring about even more innovative ways of dealing with them. You can observe this with more or less amusement in the case of Italian car thieves and American computer hackers. You strengthen what you fight against.

It is far from rare for such a spiral to lead to the complete breakdown of the relationship of trust. Everyone knows a story of how mistrust has destroyed a relationship. An old idea:

123

Whatever we restrict the freedom of strives to break out. It's a mistake to believe we can bind a person with fetters (be they made of iron, money or paper). And if our prisoner were to remain, what would be gained? Peace results from defeats in battles that it would be disastrous to win.

Mistrust is a self-fulfilling prophecy. The tighter you make the room for manoeuvre, the more likely rules are to be broken. The smaller the implicit contract, the more likely agreements are to be broken. If the employee wants to move at all within narrow confines, they have to break the rules. The manager perceives this as a breach of trust and exploits the disappointment in order to increase regulation still further.

Another thing we often see: mistrustful managers like talking about trust (instead of expectations, which would be better) and they suddenly and surprisingly become passive. They make a seamless transition from over-responsibility to under-responsibility. A lot of staff are then overstretched, make mistakes and become confused, which encourages a lot of managers: we need regulation! And as these rules require monitoring, managers suddenly find that their own behaviour changes, since they have to monitor adherence to the rules. They have succeeded in making a mess.

Mistrust thrives on abuse of trust. That's why Robert K. Merton wrote: "Mistrustful managers will always find that staff subsequently justify their mistrust by their behaviour." We see the two tendencies that are so typical in the trust dilemma: there is the desire to see trust confirmed that also prevents such confirmation because of the expectation of disappointment. There are people with a sophisticated cynical attitude who positively revel in their disappointment. One more quotation from Seneca: "Some people have taught others to cheat because they fear being cheated."

An example: when my son was 16, he worked in a warehouse during his summer holidays. In a brief interview beforehand, most of the questions revolved around theft: "What do you think about stealing? Have you ever stolen anything? What would you do if you saw another member of staff stealing something?" Staff were searched on a random basis. There were big notices on the walls: "We report every instance of theft." When I asked him how the staff reacted to the checks, my son said: "They get on their nerves to such an extent that they make a sport out of stealing goods and getting them past the checkpoints. Some of them just leave the goods behind the checkpoints."

The self-fulfilling prophecy, which has been confirmed again and again by research, gives us an important warning: *Mistrust someone and they will confirm your mistrust*. A person who isn't trusted feels unable to convince the other person that they are trustworthy. Mistrust positively encourages people to be dishonest. Why be honest when the other person has decided I am dishonest anyway? Why confirm trust when the other person mistrusts me anyway?

Trust is the better method. It may seem more sensible to be pessimistic. But once you start to mistrust, you don't need to do anything else: you will produce the phenomenon that you complain about afterwards and experience yourself to be a victim of. I shall say this because it is vital to me to be understood at this point: *intensified security measures not only don't replace the trust mechanism, they render it ineffective*. It may be that the pessimist avoids disgrace, but at the same time they destroy assets that have a real value in business: when trust is destroyed, more is lost than just trust.

When you trust, there is a good chance that the member of staff will prove trustworthy and justify your trust. This won't happen with mistrust. If you mistrust someone, they can never prove they are able and willing to confirm trust. With trust you may win or lose; with mistrust you always lose.

You can see this in your private life: the person who is aware that the other person is unpredictable and therefore expects failure from the start enters the relationship with the handbrake on, as it were. They start the relationship with a reservation about security. They won't really get involved, they won't give themselves – and they won't experience the joys of giving themselves. They might as well not even begin because their reservation prevents the possibility of the relationship flourishing. Because they don't want to lose, they can't win. With their mistrust they bring about the behaviour that they subsequently complain about. If they trust, they can't be sure that things will go well. If they distrust, they can be sure that things will go wrong.

Shakespeare's Othello asks Iago for "ocular proof" of Desdemona's unfaithfulness. That's easy for Iago: doubt is an insidious poison. Mistrust always becomes the source of its own proof. Conversely, it would have been more difficult, virtually impossible, to furnish ocular proof of Desdemona's faithfulness. By her killing herself? Trust can't be positively proven. One trusts because there is no evidence that one shouldn't trust. That is what makes trust vulnerable. Really deep mistrust is virtually impossible to eradicate. It leads to behaviour that supports the validity of mistrust. It soon becomes impossible to know whether mistrust was ever justified. It has brought about the reality that it controls. It has fulfilled itself. It is now rational. But in any case, it prevents people trying the alternative and experimenting with trust. However, if you don't trust trust and mistrust mistrust, you'll never find out whether trust would have been justified. Mistrust and excessive control mean there is no opportunity for someone to prove trustworthy. So trust begins when you act *as though* you trust.

You can't have a world without surprises. Everybody knows the only certainties are death and taxes. Maximum security destroys what we need for economic success. We need just the level of security to ensure that what we are doing doesn't come to grief simply because of one error. It is enough, however, to stay within the domain of sensible self-preservation. Trust is therefore nowadays the permanent reinterpretation of the relationship appropriate in each case between explicit and implicit contract, control and relinquishment of control, rule and exception, duty of care and responsibility.

This isn't an invitation to a suicide party. It isn't a challenge to run through oilfields with a flaming torch. But we need to organize our companies in such a way that they can't be set on fire with a single match. We don't need security neurosis, just a minimum degree of security so as not to encourage the bad guys. Apart from that, we can import what security experts recommend for different situations; it's better to work out a crisis reaction plan than to try to cover yourself against all eventualities. That's why it's best not to take a hotel room above the ninth floor. If it comes down to it, the fire brigade's ladders don't reach any higher.

*"At the end of the day Cain brought of the fruit of the ground an
offering unto the Lord. And Abel, he brought of the firstling
of his flock and of the fat thereof.*

*And the Lord had respect unto Abel and to his offering, but unto
Cain and to his offering he had not respect.*

And Cain was very wroth, and his countenance fell....

*And while they were in the field, Cain attacked his brother Abel
and slew him."*

An ancient scene: two brothers made sacrifices, and one was accepted by God and the other rejected. Then came the terrible deed,
fratricide. Some readers may ask: "What on earth is this? What
does it have to do with trust?" I want to draw your attention to a
feeling that tends to be repressed; it has been entirely ignored so far
in management literature, but it explains the reactions to a refusal
to trust, or downright mistrust. I'm talking about the experience of
shame. The thoughts I'm about to explain derive largely from an
interpretation by Till Bastian and Micha Hilgers of the parable of
Cain and Abel in the Old Testament.

When you sacrifice something, you forgo it in order to get
something else that appears valuable to you. You make a contribution first because you expect something. That's risky. Not every
sacrifice is honoured. This situation is similar to trust. Trust too
doesn't come without a price. When you confirm trust, you also do
without something. You forgo the advantage that you could have had
if you had exploited the other person's trust. You have let the chance
go by. That is your cost. But not every investment is profitable.

Put yourself in the position of a member of staff for a
moment. Imagine you consider yourself trustworthy, you look for

co-operation on the basis of mutual respect, you'd like to be recognized by your manager as a person of integrity, and you approach your manager in that spirit. The two brothers Cain and Abel also approached a higher authority trusting that they would be accepted in a benevolent way. They would like their sacrifice to be accepted. And then the incomprehensible happens: Cain's sacrifice is spurned. There is no obvious reason. In any case, God doesn't tell him. Cain feels he has been rejected for no reason; he has a profound feeling of shame. He is completely helpless; he can't do anything to induce God to accept his sacrifice. He sees only one way to escape his sense of shame, to regain the initiative, to restore his dignity. He will transform shame into guilt through fratricide.

We all fear rejection, being cut off, degradation. We want to be secure, we want to belong, we want to encounter trust and goodwill. Cain too had this desire for security: he was vulnerable, he needed protection, he didn't want to feel cut off, he hoped to find God's favour when he made his sacrifice. He trusted that his sacrifice would be accepted. But evidently the grace of God works by mysterious laws. He rejects the offering without even saying why. Cain can't see what else he can do; he doesn't know what he has done wrong. And this is precisely why the experience is so wounding and he feels so helpless. What does he do? He turns passivity into activity. He exchanges shame for guilt. It's easier for him to deal with guilt than shame. Why? In his sense of shame, he doesn't even know what he should have done differently. He clearly doesn't meet God's expectation, but he doesn't know what His expectation is. With the experience of guilt he has a choice: after all, he could refrain from the action. He does something forbidden. That is preferable for him: a state of powerlessness and helplessness is so hard to bear that he would rather flee into criminality. And then his rejection means something to him, it is comprehensible.

129

Shame is *uncomprehended* rejection. We're unable to do something, we are not what we are expected to be, we are evidently wrong. Something is beyond our control. We are victims, we suffer. When we feel ashamed, we don't want to be seen, we remain silent, we can neither ask nor speak. Shame means humiliation and loss of respect.

Guilt is *comprehended* rejection. We do something forbidden, something we could have decided not to do. Then things are within our control: we are the doer, we have chosen the situation. When we are guilty we are seen, we are no longer dumbfounded, we can defend ourselves, we can speak, we may even be able to ask why we were rejected. Then at least we know why we are wrong.

The exchange of shame for guilt. The same thing happens when we are met with fundamental mistrust: with individual suspicion on the part of our manager or colleagues, or with structural suspicion through the many institutionalized symbols of mistrust in companies. When we are rejected in a way that is incomprehensible, when we receive the message "I don't trust you" everywhere, either openly or subliminally, when we are not recognized as a partner capable of making agreements, when the other person takes precautions in case we are dishonest, when we see the monitoring procedures, when we sense that the eye of the higher authority is looking on us in a way that isn't benevolent, when we consider ourselves to be trustworthy and don't know why the other person is keeping us under surveillance all the same: that's difficult to endure. Our sense of self-worth is injured, we feel we aren't understood, we are convinced we aren't being seen properly. Just as the primeval force of shame drove Cain to a crime because that was easier for him to deal with, so we will look for ways and means to combat the experience of powerlessness. We do that by exercising a preference for the forbidden action rather than the feeling of helplessness.

Then we prefer to confirm the mistrust; at least we know why we are rejected. That's exactly what people do when society gives them no opportunity to feel needed, to make a contribution, to be welcome as a member, so they turn to right-wing extremism. That's precisely what happens when someone is dismissed, is rejected by his boss, doesn't know why someone else is preferred to him and finally goes on a rampage and kills his boss and colleagues. It's also what happens when a perfectly normal member of staff senses that he isn't trusted, has no chance of proving himself trustworthy, has no opportunity to confirm trust because it has been denied him from the beginning, and so only uses his scope for discretion to his own advantage.

The murderous or suicidal consequences that follow when we don't trust our staff and don't confirm the trust they have placed in us – that's something our rejected brother Cain can teach us.

The artificial limbs of trust

How do you get people to do what you want? How do you make people's behaviour predictable? How do you overcome fear? Many people need reasons to trust. But these reasons can't come from a person you distrust. That's why you resort to the artificial limbs of trust.

Agreements on targets

People keep claiming that agreement on targets create commitment, but I have fundamental doubts about them (see *Aufstand des Individuums* [Revolt of the Individual], 2000), even though they are useful within their limited scope. I'd like to amplify these doubts from the point of view of the economics of trust. First of all, if we are honest, agreements on targets are born of mistrust. They were invented when people lost their bearings, when they no longer had face-to-face contact or the means to check whether the other person was fully engaging himself. Or because someone was dissatisfied with the performance of a member of staff, because someone wanted to add impetus, because something was needed in writing to make it possible to reward and punish more effectively (or the other way around: because people wanted to protect themselves against arbitrary superiors).

If we leave aside the fundamentals, the main thing is *how* the targets have come about. If they are imposed from above, you are right to be mistrustful as to whether a member of staff is really doing everything to achieve them. However, if the targets have been negotiated in a two-way process, you should allow the member of staff to choose how to achieve them and trust that they will be achieved. If you also announce a bonus for achieving the targets, you send out a signal of mistrust and provision in case of non-achievement. You don't achieve adherence to agreements in this way.

If market conditions deteriorate and performance possibilities disappear, you have to trust the member of staff to approach you on his own initiative to negotiate a different agreement if a target no longer seems achievable. Saying "That wasn't much good" at the end of a year will set the spiral of mistrust into operation. However, it will also come into operation if you don't take the member of staff seriously and add an extra 20 percent margin to proposed targets in the negotiations so that you can get your way with the targets you really have in mind. This is something deeply ingrained in the minds of many managers: a policy of dictating targets, setting them as high as possible and regularly increasing them to keep people under constant pressure.

As an instrument, agreements on targets will never solve the problems of mistrust. The reason is clear: negotiating, agreeing and reviewing targets require trust. People need to assume that the other party is serious and operating from a position of honesty. But this is precisely what doesn't happen with the practice of target agreements. Ask yourself: do you set working targets in a dictatorial way? Are your expectations so ambitious that they are achievable only under exceptionally favourable conditions? Or are they set in such a way that people may well exceed them so that you can feel pleased about it?

However you answer these questions, our earlier discussion about the binding effect of trust throws a much clearer light on target agreements as a management tool. Their binding effect is weak, as every practical person will agree. They open the door to degrading victim stories with their "money or no money" mechanism. They are tied to the idea of stability: circumstances remaining the same as they were at the time of the agreement. They reckon with a breach of the agreement by way of provision.

Trust is different: it expects people to stick by agreements. It doesn't call the other person's integrity into doubt. It doesn't build a refuge by way of provision. And people pick up on that. This is something to be noted by the pessimistic kettledrums in the orchestra pits of companies who think any alternative ideas are unrealistic:

It isn't target agreements that create commitment; it is trust.

To illustrate this I'll recount a story told to me by Götz W. Werner, CEO of the drugstore chain dm. The cook on a fishing boat told the apprentice cook to take a cup of coffee up to the captain on the bridge every morning at 10 a.m. So the objective was set and clearly defined. When the apprentice returned from his first mission, he said, "I got told off because the coffee had slopped over. But that's no surprise at wind force nine!" "Then don't fill the cup so full," said the cook. The boy did as he was told next morning. "I got told off again," he said, "because the cup wasn't quite full." "I don't know what to do," said the cook, "you think of something." The next day, the cook asked "What happened this time?" "All fine," said the boy. "I filled the cup to the brim, took a sip, walked up to the door, spat the coffee back into the cup, and then he told me I was a good boy."

When we trust someone, we trust they will do the right thing under the circumstances, whatever those circumstances may be. When we trust someone, we assume they will be flexible and sensible in different situations, and even solve unforeseen problems. We trust that they will use their room for discretion to our benefit. When we distrust, we don't assume that. We aren't sure whether they will operate in such a way as to solve problems. When we don't trust, we feel the necessity to guarantee the other person's behaviour. But such a guarantee isn't built into target agreements (nor is it with any rule). If rules are to work, we need confidence in someone's goodwill and belief that their conduct will be appropriate to situations as they arise. If we have that confidence, it isn't the rules that we are trusting.

As circumstances are always changing and rules can never cover all eventualities, we need to adapt rules constantly. That's an expensive process. Rules need interpretation and conditions of application. The reality is more than the words. Let's take the stormy sea from the fishing boat story as a symbol for turbulent markets: target agreements may be helpful in calm waters (for example, when the markets are highly lucrative); they may help focus energy and act as lifebuoys on a shared journey; they may even balance expectations in a sensible way. But if the cost of renegotiating them seems too high when markets are turbulent, you have no choice: you have to jettison your target agreements. Trust is more flexible and more realistic. Then you have to be serious about the idea that "We expect everyone to do their best." That – and only that – is called commitment. And it is worthy of the term.

Marriage contracts

Any couple that has been living together without being married is sure to encounter scepticism. People will say "You aren't showing each other any commitment." "We know men who read books about divorce before they even get married." "They haven't really decided on each other." Although I don't know many people who find married life fantastic (most of them *were* married once), a lot of unmarried people feel got at by married people. Snide remarks are made over and over again: "When are they going to get round to getting married?" Do they want to drag others down into that life? Are they opposed to the unconventional? Or do they have an inner sense about what we explain here when we talk about the trust mechanism?

In his book *Democracy in America*, Alexis de Tocqueville says, "A loving relationship between unmarried people is punished quite strongly. The judge was empowered to inflict a pecuniary penalty, a whipping, or marriage." Some people insist on choosing the fine or flogging. They follow Mae West: "Marriage is an institution, and I ain't ready for an institution yet." When people marry in Germany, the advertisement often says *Wir trauen uns*. This statement carries three meanings: first, we have courage; second, we trust each other; and third, we are getting married. The sense of relief is unmistakable and universal: "Now they are sure, now they have confidence in each other."

Is that so? Every man and woman knows that a wedding has as much to do with marriage as bringing up children has to do with OshKosh clothes. And if marriage is about promising each other security and staying together on the lifelong path from the courting couple on the park bench to the two wise old people on rocking-chairs on the veranda, then why is it that so many people are unhappy and get divorced? If we look at the divorce rates, marriage long ago ceased to be a safe haven. Is this moral decline? Is it just a postmodern game of musical chairs? Does marriage owe its poor image to the fact that it has been distorted for romantic reasons throughout history? Could it be that marriage doesn't create but actually weakens the basis for a lifelong partnership?

This is my theory: marriage doesn't involve giving trust; on the contrary, it destroys trust. A hidden psychological dynamic undermines what is supposed to be evoked.

Of course, it is a suspended sentence. This becomes easier to understand (even if it doesn't make it any easier for many people to agree with it) if we take a closer look at the trust mechanism. After all, trust is the basis for living together without any contractual regulation. The partners have few if any mutual legal rights. The biggest consequence of a breach of trust is that they will no longer live together. Even if people promise each other eternal love, even if they make arrangements and agree on rules, in terms of the psychology of contracts, living together without being married is an *implicit contract*. The content of this implicit contract is (as we have shown above) threefold. First, we keep to the agreed rules and arrangements. Second, we refrain from explicit control and security measures. Third, we conduct ourselves in accordance with the spirit of our relationship. If the implicit contract is to remain effective, the partners must confirm trust again and again. They have to make an effort for each other.

Now, an essential factor in trust is that it can be abused. The other person may end the relationship at any time (termination being easier, at least in the formal sense, than it is in a marriage). This form of living together is therefore risky; it makes people vulnerable. And it is precisely this vulnerability that *creates commitment*. It creates entitlement. It binds. It has a constructive force that results from the free nature of voluntary commitment. And the greater the vulnerability, the greater the binding effect.

The important thing is this: trust has a far greater binding effect than an explicit contract ever could.

You can see this especially when the partners don't want to be dependent on each other: *when trust is replaced by explicit security measures.*

If we take an objective look at marriage, this network of precepts and prohibitions and rights of mutual exploitation is essentially born of fear. Marriage was invented for unfortunate times.

The form of marriage prevalent today developed from a problematic situation in the Middle Ages. A little history: today's legal arrangements for marriage are a by-product of the Crusades. The noble knight left his house, wife and child to defend the Holy Land against the unbelievers (and to make his fortune at the same time). Often he was never seen again. In those days, couples spent between 12 and 15 years together before one of them was carried off by war or illness. The estates, the main source of income for the families who remained, were deprived of protection if the knight didn't return home. It became difficult for the wife and children to assert their rights against the economically stronger and ambitious though still dependent people. It was unclear which goods were subject to duty and which weren't. It occurred to people that the rights and duties, ownership and estates of those who were left behind could be written down before the knight set off for the east so that legal rights could be established. This was done in a book, and the book was in the church. The form of wedding we know today developed in this way with the assistance of the Catholic church.

So marriage was originally intended to protect the rights of knights' families in the case of absence or death at the time of the Crusades. Its function today is similar, except that now a succession of partners has taken the place of the Crusades, and when love has gone the state has jurisdiction over money and children. Marriage is a patriarchal, feudal contract: sex, housekeeping and child-rearing in exchange for security, food and clothing. Even the love-match is a fashion, invented 175 years ago.

But irrespective of the individual reasons for marriage – love, security, tradition, romance, commitment, tax advantages – marriage is not just a symbol of belonging together, but a fundamental qualitative turning point. To speak plainly: it is the *breaking of the implicit contract*. Marriage replaces an implicit contract with an explicit one. It replaces one's own responsibility with an externally located responsible person. It replaces trust with apparent security. It replaces weak ties with a legally enforceable contract. It replaces trust-based commitment with the threat of punishment.

The breach of the implicit contract is more felt than understood, but the consequences are far-reaching. The binding effect of lived trust is absent, and people don't feel so deeply committed. Mutual trust no longer has to be justified or confirmed again and again. The partners no longer feel they have to make such an effort for each other as they did during the time of relative vulnerability. Small disrespectful acts mount up. Some couples embark on the long, slow path to silence. Many partners feel positively encouraged to be unfaithful because the inner psychological costs of a bad conscience cease to apply when there is a mutual withdrawal of trust.

Paradoxically, many couples react to the deterioration in the state of the marriage with an intensification of agreements and controls. But we know that control systems work only until ways are found to circumvent them. Marriage seems to be a formal justification for unfaithfulness. Sometimes a woman may be relieved that her lover is marrying someone else: then she knows she can keep him.

If you don't trust your own worth, if you don't believe your partner will stay with you because they want you, if you aren't sure there is a balance of give and take, then you will try to chain the other person. If you are jealous, or feel you aren't worthy of the other person, then you have lost trust *in yourself*. Just imagine how it would be if the other person were to stay with you: could anything be worse? As I've already said, there are battles it would be disastrous to win.

Now, you may insist that people have to trust each other even in marriage. Agreed. But trust is no longer the *core* of the contract in the relationship. People couch moral arguments in the form of "should" sentences simply because trust is less fundamental and because the necessity isn't there. Trust doesn't work well as a wagging finger; it's much better as an economic mechanism, as I hope I've shown.

My theory is this: the idea of entering into marriage on the basis of fear will be rejected with great indignation, especially by those who wish to defend their past. What isn't allowed to be can't be. Even those readers who are able to follow the reasoning presented here will find it rather unpleasant. But that doesn't make it wrong. Please bear in mind that I'm not talking about legal arguments, unfair or despicable behaviour or socio-political structures. My argument is this: marriage doesn't create security, it hinders it. *Love is a tender thread, not a fetter.* The trust mechanism that effectively binds two unmarried people to each other is destroyed by the explicit contract of marriage. Marriage breaks trust, and the phenomena we complain about are covertly created. The great philosopher Hegel warned his contemporaries against mixing love and marriage. He probably knew the reason: the secret of a good partnership is awareness of its vulnerability.

What prevents us trusting

It is generally assumed that rational behaviour in companies should encourage action based on trust. Before we turn to this subject, we should take an objective look at what hinders trust. This is because there are some problematic conditions that prevent a culture of trust.

Limited freedom of choice

First of all, it is legitimate only to trust behaviour that is fundamentally suitable to a relationship of trust. When companies such as FedEx, Deere, Harley-Davidson, S.C. Johnson Wax and Southwest Airlines announce "no layoffs" policies, they are either not in the market, blind or dishonest: they promise something that can't be promised, and that therefore doesn't deserve trust. In Germany, workers believed for a long time in companies run in the patriarchal way that protected them from the harsh winds of globalization. Then in the early nineties, many of these traditional companies began sacking workers, which many people interpreted, wrongly, as an abuse of trust by management. But the workers should never have given that trust. Under competitive conditions, job security can't be the object of a contract. It's dishonest to make people believe that something in their life is secure. Security is an illusion, fortunately.

Moreover, as a matter of principle, there must be *freedom of choice* in a relationship of trust. This is necessary on *both* sides: the choice of giving or not giving trust on the one side, and the choice of confirming or disappointing trust on the other. As a manager, when you trust, you presume that your member of staff won't exploit your co-operative behaviour. That's why you don't restrict their choice of action. If, however, you do restrict their scope of action, there isn't much room for trust. If the employee's scope for action is so tiny, so regulated, so hedged in that they have no opportunity to disappoint your expectations, then they can't choose this option. The situation produces no binding effect for the member of staff. Movement needs room. And room needs trust. And trust requires freedom.

Niklas Luhmann put it like this: "You can't trust a sovereign." Someone who comes across as inviolable, unapproachable and invulnerable – someone who presents themselves as supreme – doesn't acquire trust *precisely for that reason*. For companies, this means that no one can ask for trust in a credible way without actively having made themselves vulnerable.

So the employee must have the choice of confirming or disappointing trust. If near-total control of action is possible, trust has no role to play. If you aren't at all vulnerable, there is no implicit contract between you and your staff. Without vulnerability, trust is redundant. For example, in the case of piecework, there is almost total control of work performance via the result. In typing pools, workers can be given a reminder if their computer keyboards have been unused for more than 30 seconds. In such cases, a breach of trust on the part of the employee will not be seriously detrimental to the manager. So we can't talk about a risk on your part that has a binding effect on your staff.

At the same time, however, a relationship of trust requires you as the manager to have freedom of choice. You must have the option to say no to a relationship based on co-operation. You must be able to limit your risk. You have three basic options for this:

1   Choose not to enter into a relationship based on co-operation in the first place.
2   Terminate it.
3   Reduce the risk by means of security systems or restricting scope for action.

If you go for option 3, you can't avoid the rising costs of a spiral of mistrust, as we have already shown. This is why options 1 and 2 need to be open: ending the co-operation or not entering into it in the first place. However, if external conditions block or prohibit these options, 3 is the only alternative, with all the consequences it involves.

Normally, people who don't trust each other end their relationship. Logically, this is in both their interests in the long term. But it isn't so easy in the world of work. Highly regulated relationships prevent or hinder freedom of movement. One can see how nonsensical the restriction of freedom of choice or extension of the explicit contract is by looking at the protection against dismissal that exists in Germany. It is excessive, although ostensibly beneficial for employees. Not only does it prevent severance, but it dictates that the ones to go first must be the very young (cheap) and the very old (subsidized). The result: the binding effect that comes from freedom hardly operates. An attenuated form of this mechanism is found in many companies' efforts to use money to retain staff who want to change jobs. This is a disservice. It replaces the implicit contract with an extended explicit one. It replaces personal commitment with golden handcuffs. It replaces the particular with the general. It replaces that which truly binds with that which makes the basis of the manager/employee relationship replaceable.

If a member of staff can end an employment relationship but a manager can't, or only at a prohibitively high cost, then a relationship based on trust can't develop. The greater the explicit contract that restricts mutual freedom of choice, the more superfluous trust is. The inability to terminate the relationship disables the trust mechanism. The economics of trust show one thing clearly and I'm not afraid to say it: *trust plays no role under the co-operative conditions of the civil service.*

Trust requires the freedom to choose and the ability to avoid co-operation. It seems paradoxical, but it is only the partners' ability to switch that creates the conditions for potential long-term relationships. Trust binds. If you can't choose to decline co-operation, you don't have a choice. And if you can't avoid co-operation, mistrust and all its mechanical consequences will follow. And so it becomes clear yet again: trust isn't moral action. It doesn't necessarily consist in believing in the other person's good intentions. It can be assigned to the rational sphere. It consists of a rational policy of maximizing benefit, an intelligence that calculates advantage. You can *decide* to trust. As givers of trust, we all have to make calculated decisions about investing trust. And as recipients of trust, we must decide whether the trust given is to be honoured. If we are to give a fair account of the consequences of actions in the company, we don't have to poke around in people's morals and intentions. We don't have to beg people to stick to agreements. We can at last abandon the coercive mindset that pervades so many undignified company rituals and personnel systems. And we prevent people from being morally overtaxed. If we assess actions not on the basis of the intentions behind them but in terms of their consequences, then even a radical moral egotist will find it difficult to be correct in their conduct.

The extent to which trust, freedom and responsibility are interconnected in practice is highlighted by some interesting results of an Allensbach study carried out in autumn 1999. Of those people who experienced a high degree of freedom at their place of work and confirmed that they were shown a lot of trust, 54 percent didn't take a single day off sick. Of those who didn't have much sense of freedom or experience much trust, just 23 percent attended work every day. Effects on the attachment to work could be identified. One test identified individuals' attitudes from their advice in a particular situation. There were two colleagues, both working on an assignment that had to be finished the next morning. When one of them had finished his contribution at the end of the day, he noticed that his colleague had gone home without finishing his work. Individuals were asked whether they thought he should finish his colleague's work so that the assignment would be completed. Among respondents who experienced a high degree of freedom at their place of work, 69 percent said "He should finish his colleague's work." However, among those who didn't feel much freedom the figure was only 28 percent.

This is confirmed in practice again and again: when you trust people, they move from a duty of care to a sense of responsibility, from the explicit to the implicit contract. Then you can trust them to act from a sense of commitment even in unusual situations.

It isn't only in times of giant mergers that the feeling of having no power or influence is one of the biggest threats to trust. In organizations that are too big to allow an overview and lack a human dimension, the last vestiges of familiarity wither. We see relationships that make it almost impossible for people to take responsibility for the success of the overall operation. The sense of being a cog in a wheel, the attitude of "What difference can I make?" are the consequences when people feel their own contribution is meaningless. Feelings of anonymity, disconnectedness and hierarchy develop. And conditions that favour trust perish, together with other delicate entities such as self-determination.

A feeling of powerlessness often predominates even in everyday situations: "My boss is demanding overtime, so I have to do it. Otherwise he'll transfer me to another department, or else I'll be the victim of the next phase of restructuring." "The board has decided, so I have no choice." People often experience themselves as powerless in relation to their superiors. The same applies between companies when a more powerful partner drives the other to the wall. For example, VW under Jose Ignacio Lopez was sometimes so ruthless in its search for cost-effective suppliers that the supplier community is still tainted by a deep-seated feeling of mistrust.

Power is present in all areas of life and society. When two people come together, a power structure is established as an automatic reflex. But how does power come to power? It is not innate in those who have it. They are only powerful as long as there is someone to whom they can give orders. In his famous passage about master and slave in *Phenomenology of Spirit*, the great philosopher Hegel tried to explain that it is actually the slave who has power. He can look for another master. Without the slave, the master is no longer a master. Power always requires two parties: one who exercises power and one who allows it. To put it differently, power is always only lent. Even companies are to a large extent open organizations. It is possible to join and leave; you can decide to withdraw completely from life *in* the company and even withdraw (albeit not completely) from a life *with* companies.

So power is not a fixed institution or structure; it is defined every time between people in specific situations with their requirements, obstacles, players and boundary conditions. The role of the powerless person is traditionally always ascribed to the member of staff. However, if we look at the statistics, many more employees leave their employer than *vice versa*. This leaves a tyrannical boss looking like a garden gnome from a reject shop. So power doesn't come from above. It exists in the relationship of one individual to another insofar as the individual has freedom to act. Under economic conditions, power is defined by supply and demand in the changing relationships and constant interactions between the participants. Consequently, in terms of a system, it doesn't make sense to ask who influences whom and who has more power. The communication process is circular. Should we trust nevertheless?

Competition

"Believe me," said Bertram Reuss, "this business is fantastic." He was sitting in his São Paulo hotel room chairing a telephone conference spanning three time zones. He had just been appointed to the second level below the executive board and was regarded by many as a shooting star. Some colleagues regarded him as a ruthless careerist. He had been working on an acquisition for over eight months, and knew it was hugely important for his company's expansion plans and for the chairman of the board. Now was the time to act. A deadline had been set for bids for the acquisition, which was worth several million euros. Reuss sensed that his colleagues were hesitant. He hadn't given them enough time to check the documents. He was notorious for setting extremely tight deadlines to raise the pressure for decisions. But his colleagues raised questions about the validity of the figures and about cultural differences and market opportunities. After hours of arduous debate, they agreed to the bid even though their concerns hadn't been dispelled. What Reuss didn't know was that what he was bidding for had been awarded to his main competitor that morning. He was too late.

New production concepts and worldwide co-operation place big demands on an individual's subjectivity and self-management. The old control paradigm, which was supposed to eliminate subjectivity, isn't up to the job. People can only work together quickly and efficiently if they trust each other. And trust is, as we've seen, both a prerequisite for and a consequence of co-operation. This trust is initially based on people in the company or working group co-operating, supporting and informing each other, and refraining from using joint success for personal benefit. This means that the relevant values and objectives need to be shared by all. If trust is confirmed, people are encouraged to take further steps in increasing trust. Jill Pages, a member of the six-person working group Flying Pages, put it like this: "You are not really a member of the group until you have earned the trust of the others. And trust develops when you place the objective of the group above your own ego. The group always comes first." (*Fast Company*, 8, 2001, p. 46.)

Logically, co-operation should strengthen trusting behaviour, or at least one would think so. Conversely, individual traits such as unreliability, dishonesty or disloyalty are a hindrance. However, a particular hindrance is the principle of *competition* that is so pronounced in our culture, especially in the gender that dominates companies: for men, competition is the only thing for which there is no competition. Male competitive behaviour frequently reaches the level of battles for hierarchical position that you might see among packs of animals. (Incidentally, the group Flying Pages mentioned above consists of five women and one man.) It's competitive men who are generally assumed to be performance-oriented and motivated to achieve results. This need to achieve results doesn't normally include the creation of trust – and when it comes to the social dilemma between individual and collective interests, the former wins out every time.

Hierarchy gives structural support for a competitive orientation. It makes more or less all members of an organization into rivals. They are all vying for something that's in short supply: positions that the system awards to the victors. Competition is defined as a zero-sum game: the victory of one person means defeat for the other. The hierarchical bottleneck strongly encourages the individual to win the struggle for differentiation and at least look better than his colleague. Moreover, under competitive conditions mistrust is intelligent behaviour. People will be less likely to lend each other a helping hand. Why should I share my knowledge with my rival?

The increase in competitive forms of management encourages an ethos where at worst each member regards himself as a profit centre. If employees are concerned only with their own success, there's a danger they will exploit the conditions of trust. Highly individualized remuneration systems don't exactly encourage people to engage in trusting co-operation. Without a doubt, asking for entrepreneurialism will mean that people will exploit their own organization. And when hierarchies are dismantled with the help of consultants, the bottleneck is exacerbated: flat hierarchies reduce career opportunities. The quartile rule worsens things still further: the lowest 25 percent on the performance scale are in danger of being dropped. Employees don't know whether they are included, which makes all colleagues into adversaries.

At the same time, spurred on by ever-changing management trends, senior management make transformation permanent. Middle managers are given a hint that they'll be up for higher jobs if they show willingness to co-operate with change. Career competition within the company inevitably increases. Anyone who recommends abolishing hierarchies to make communication easier, even if they act from the best intentions, will actually make indirect competitors into direct ones. And the fewer higher positions that are available, the more losers will be created. Some people may argue that flat organizations do away with classical hierarchies, so that there is no competition for positions. But they overlook the fact that competition doesn't cease, but is just shifted onto another plane: the level of symbolic differences, financial distribution and opportunities to get involved with interesting projects.

The ideological claim that competition and the struggle for survival are the dominant structure for all life (as seen in the animal kingdom) has long been refuted by biologists. Nevertheless, the idea that a moderate level of competition is helpful can hardly be disputed. The problem lies in the mix of co-operation and competition. There is a distinction, as Robert Hinde pointed out, between outshining a competitor and stabbing him.

What is to be done to strengthen co-operation?

Externally, in relation to customers, money is used to answer this question, as, for example, when it is invested in advertising.

Inwardly, in relation to staff, less generosity is mustered. Staff are usually served with unappealing dishes such as corporate culture, vision and identification. Or glossy brochures are adorned with such words as "Team." But that's not enough. Companies are geared to *co-operation*. They depend on horizontal trust between people whose jobs involve producing goods and achieving goals. We must therefore give serious thought to what strengthens co-operation.

A lack of goods and an excess of needs inevitably make individuals into competitors, despite their best intentions. We can't all be encouraging fathers, friendly mothers and supportive siblings all of the time. Our interests inevitably conflict. Good behaviour doesn't simply come from within, it must be brought about by circumstances. What brings us together, what induces us to act considerately, is *common problems*. As Volker Gerhardt pointed out, apart from personal connections and sexual attraction, the only time we have anything to do with each other is when we have common problems. Co-operation emerges from communication about problems that we recognize as *common* problems and that we are able and willing to solve only *together*. A sense of connection with others comes about only through tasks that evoke commitment in everyone. If there are no questions, there can be no search for an answer. This is a mechanism that brings about communication even between adversaries: I am capable of engaging positively with my fiercest competitor when it comes to solving a common problem. But the problem to be solved must be perceived by the individual to be greater than the personal advantages of pursuing a career.

Problems that allow us to co-operate must fulfil at least two conditions. First, they must be *important* problems that affect our business life directly or indirectly. Second, they must be *self-evident* problems; it's no good if people aren't aware of them unless they are given a briefing, or unless they have a university education. The organization should be set up on this basis. Most companies have the organization first, and then the problems follow.

Trust is therefore *rational* against a background of common problems. The attitude is this: even though opposing interests are at stake, I am striving for a common understanding of the problems, wanting to understand the other person, abiding by commitments, not exploiting my scope for action to the detriment of the other person and being prepared to make compromises. Work experienced as meaningful is always work for others. A company whose staff work only *with* each other and not *for* each other will fail in the end. You'll succeed in business life if you help others get what they want. It's simple, it's obvious, and yet it's so easy to forget.

It is therefore necessary to design the company as a problem-solving society with regard to a future to be jointly created. This is important so that the company has a future. Everything that promotes solidarity is helpful, such as making sure a company isn't so big that people become alienated. Everything that divides is not helpful, such as profit centres.

Here are some questions you can use as a guide:

- Do I need the other person? Do we need each other?
- How can we make sure that success is experienced as success for all of us, and failure as failure for all of us?
- What disadvantage do I incur if things don't go well for the other person?
- What advantage do I enjoy if things do go well for the other person?

Community, a sense of ourselves and a *collective identity* can develop from the answers to these questions.

Collective identity certainly doesn't mean weakening people's individual responsibility and accountability. Indiscriminate group mentality is a degenerate form. Collective identity arises when management succeeds in presenting problems as *collective* problems. Management will only be able to do this in the long term on the basis of tested credibility. Trust is everything here. So anyone who wants to make space for the trust mechanism in the company should at least refrain from stirring up competitive energy, which is already present in abundance. This is the guiding principle:

Minimize competition, maximize co-operation.

In view of these considerations, it's obvious that it is sometimes better to choose women for positions in which values are determined. I'd like to share a few thoughts about this idea.

Digression: Women have everything required for management

"I suppose we'll have to get used to that," said the man next to me on the evening flight to Düsseldorf. He said it half to me and half into his newspaper. I muttered and nodded in agreement. Get used to what? "Captain Nicole Brackmann and her crew would like to welcome you on board." A woman! We're being flown by a woman!

People are concerned about a woman pilot. Who worries about a male pilot? Women evidently don't enjoy the trust that men receive in this area. Is it because a woman pilot is unusual? Or does the reason go deeper? What are women not trusted to do? Won't they be strong enough to operate a control lever? Will they not move the elevator decisively enough? While the plane is waiting in the stack, will they do a few extra loops just for fun?

No, of course we know that men can boast only superior strength, and that otherwise evolution has equipped women better. But this doesn't disturb the ruling men's club when it comes to management appointments. Once again, it's a question of trust: as managers, men enjoy a high degree of trust from the beginning, irrespective of the performance they achieve with their staff. Women are accepted only (if at all) when they are seen to achieve good results. Women have to prove themselves before they are recognized. A man is suitable for his occupation until he proves himself unsuitable, and even then he is kept in office by his charitable brothers. A woman is unsuitable for her job until she has proved herself suitable, and even then mistrust is always waiting to pounce.

Consequently, it is always much more risky and requires more explanation when someone wants to appoint a woman to a management position. All the more so if a woman is preferred to a man, because when the chips are down, people would rather trust a man. So anyone who decides on a woman as manager takes on a greater responsibility. The pressure for justification rises.

Once enthroned, women find things twice as difficult. There is more pressure on them to prove themselves than there is on men. In business they have to be the better man – and then people accuse them of being masculine. And as it's no longer possible to force women back into the kitchen, ridicule is the most effective means of discipline: is she quick-witted, is she tough, does she show feelings, is she a cry-baby, does she have self-control, is she an iceberg, does she work long and hard, is she married to her job, is she successful, is she a career woman. In her case, logic is interpreted as being cold and calculating, and intelligence makes her less attractive.

And yet women (especially mothers) have been waiting for years for action. Despite the difficulties, they consider life in companies desirable. But are they admitted? Working hours are frequently still rigid, and childcare provision is rare. In Germany, family policy has done nothing to encourage women to take on a challenge in working life. Just 15 percent of mothers with primary schoolchildren in western Germany have full-time jobs. They are still rare in management; in top management, they are positively exotic. You hardly ever find them right at the very top. Because they drink less? Because they don't eat so fast? Because they are not so good at parking? Kienbaum-Beratung carried out a study on income policy among 1,017 chief executives. There were just 28 women amongst them: 3 percent. The fact that they are considerably less well-paid than their male colleagues merely confirms a development that has been apparent for decades. When it comes to career, the decisive factor is neither intelligence nor performance, but self-presentation.

Does there have to be some huge demographic shift to allow women to take an active role in business life? No; it's women's specific talents that modern companies can use. Business hasn't yet realized the advantages women bring. Companies, listen: women have everything you're looking for!

Many of the management qualities needed under future economic conditions are innate in women. Over millions of years they have developed the willingness and ability to put others first and themselves second. Is there anything companies need more urgently? Women already have assets that men acquire only after great effort, things some testosterone hulks will never learn: organizational talents, integrated thinking, recognizing paradoxes and still being able to act, an understanding of a wide range of people, the ability to make decisions appropriate to situations, the ability to communicate with different listeners, multi-tasking. . . . Think of the circus trick spinning the plates. Mothers have learned to handle a staggering number of tasks brilliantly. They have learned by having to deal with children, schools, authorities, tradesmen and other service providers and balancing the double role of professional and mother as well as being the first port of call for relatives and acquaintances. They are, as Birger Priddat puts it "chief executives of Families Ltd."

Research tells us:

- While men tend to solve problems with a strategy of defeating something, women have an array of problem-solving strategies to hand and can deal with a variety of situations without producing losers. There may have been a marriage made in heaven between Daimler and Chrysler, but it was a marriage of men; did it degenerate into a virtual cultural war for that reason?

- Women naturally think in a systemic way. Take a look at men and women boarding an aircraft. Men's social IQ seems to plummet; they are either clumsy or outrageous to a risible degree. Women demonstrate a process-related intelligence: they usually look ahead, they are prudent and considerate, and they make an effort to avoid obstructing others.

- Women don't have more feelings than men. This is claimed again and again, but although it appears plausible, it is fortunately nonsense. They normally have more *contact* with their feelings; they don't push them away. In addition to the rational faculty, there is also a sensing faculty: an inner experience that speaks a language that is sometimes clearer and more in accord with reality than the apparently rational language spoken by male cognitive machines. So women are more sensitive to relationships and subliminal impressions, and can express these things. They react to early warnings that something doesn't feel right. Isn't relationship management something we need everywhere now? The way men deal with emotions borders on mental debility.

It's often said that we'll be satisfied only when as many female poor performers take up careers as male ones. These are the old battles! It isn't a question of calling women to power and negotiating quotas. That's the wrong way. Many cases where women are in the wrong job are attributable to an inexhaustible women's bonus. What we need is not proportional representation but a strategic HR policy that takes account of competence. Women aren't better or worse, they're simply *different*. They deploy gender-specific abilities, they have different things in their socio-biographic kit that can be used in a worthwhile way. Wherever a communicative approach is successful, that's where they are needed. No, I don't mean your company's PR department or customer service or sales. I mean *all* management positions in your company, your own included.

A good manager has few tasks, but competent communication is vital for them: developing strategies in a team and communicating instead of imposing, binding the most important customers and partners on a long-term basis. Conducting negotiations in which both contractual parties emerge as winners. In particular, being in constant dialogue with staff in order to create the conditions to obtain their best performance. The best team is the one that shines through the performance of the staff, not the manager.

With men, you'll seldom encounter willingness to stand in their staff's shadow.

Anyone who has the courage to act in their company's interests will have to examine why they have more trust in men.

Trusting nevertheless

If we look at the overall structural and personal conditions that have a negative effect on trust, we might be discouraged and feel like giving up. We shouldn't do that. But I do think it's dishonest to close our eyes to the negative aspects, to pass over them diplomatically or to make an ideological appeal for new heart in order to avoid them. In all our considerations, something has become clear again and again:

In companies, trust is always a case of "trusting nevertheless."

Some things would be simpler if the public preachers of trust were to take an open and honest look at the negative side and encourage people using the word "nevertheless" instead of preaching a hollow optimism that not even a schoolchild would swallow. And there are reasons for this "nevertheless." There is no reasonable alternative to a trust-based organization under future economic conditions. Moreover, there are conditions and forms of behaviour that allow trust to develop even where it has been eroded. I will deal with these now.

Managers who regard themselves as facilitators know they can't achieve success by means of control. They realize that many important things in business can't be managed, that people and organizations can't be controlled, but can be influenced. They support co-operation between people; they provide opportunities, possibilities and scope in which people can tackle the tasks they have chosen for themselves. They trust the people and the situation. They trust life. And they have to trust themselves.

That may be the hardest thing. The footnotes of commercial history are full of the names of timid managers: talented, but without courage. If managers are to be truly successful, they need to venture onto the open sea and allow themselves to lose sight of the land for a while. They must estimate the risk, face what lies beyond, confront the unfamiliar. This won't happen without surprises and shocks. When the much-admired Jack Welch of GE was asked by a freshman at Fairfield University what he thought was the most important thing in management, he said: "Self confidence! That is the most important thing. And I have learned as much from my mistakes as my successes. They complement each other and self-confidence develops." (In *c-span*, 21 August 2001.)

But what does the trust mechanism have to do with self-confidence? If we take a look at the history of language, the German word for trust (*Vertrauen*) came from the Middle High German term *trûwen*. The original meaning of the word included "hope" and "believe"; later it meant "giving trust" (*Vertrauen schenken*), and the reflexive form *Sich zutrauen* "to trust oneself" or *wagen*, "to dare." The circularity of the process is reflected in its linguistic history: you succeed in trusting only if you *trust yourself*, if you allow yourself to be vulnerable.

But you can make yourself vulnerable only when you feel secure within yourself. You need a certain degree of inner equanimity and strength *to cope with the tension between the expectation of trust and the possibility of betrayal.* If you can't do that and feel anxious, then you'll try to control the environment, make other people's reactions predictable and minimize the likelihood of disappointment. You'll span your environment with a web of security measures. If you have the fundamental conviction that you can't trust someone, you won't become convinced of the contrary even by the other person's constant trustworthy behaviour. Suspicion is your constant companion. So in the end, the willingness and capability to give and receive trust is based on individual self-confidence. Without self-confidence, it isn't possible to trust others, or even to believe in God.

Only those who trust themselves can trust others.

Self-confidence: few qualities are so high on our wish list, or more admired. It's the inner certainty that I'm reliable, I can count on myself, when I say "yes," I mean "yes." But as with trust, we often recognise self-confidence only through its absence: when we hesitate, feel despondent, quickly defer to other people's opinions, suffer because of criticism, give way to social pressure or lack initiative when decisive action is needed. When we have confidence in ourselves, we have independent judgement: we know ourselves what to believe and what to do. We take other people's views and opinions into account, but don't let them obliterate our own ideas.

Let's take an example: science has still not been able to prove that one particular diet is more healthy than another. Dietary recommendations may be plausible, but they are pointless: as much use as recommending a particular shoe size. If someone wants to live a healthy life, they have to find out for themselves what is good for them and what is harmful. This also applies to our life in a company. If you have self-confidence, trust in your own ideas will be more important to you than adapting to other people's ideas. You have confidence in your own emotional, intellectual and moral competence. You believe in your intentions and capabilities and reliability. You regard yourself as a person of integrity; you see yourself in a positive light. This is the inner absolute sense of self-esteem.

You need to be able to trust yourself in order to give a promise. You need to know yourself to be a person who doesn't have to expect surprises within yourself. In order to be responsible for your actions, you need to be able to exclude any instabilities that might emanate from the depths of your psyche. When there are surprises from outside, self-confidence includes the ability to cope with them. It involves doing what's necessary in an unexpected situation such as a breach of trust. When disappointed, you retain your composure. So self-confidence involves developing a sense of certainty that you can be responsible for your actions; above all, on a practical level it involves the experience of being capable of keeping to agreements *in the face of adversity*.

But even this is a matter of degree. The quality I'm talking about doesn't correspond to a demonstrative act of "Look out, here I come!" Self-confidence isn't a competition in which you need to outshine someone else. It's a calm, relaxed attitude that has an inner conviction that you'll survive even a breach of trust. For disappointment is inevitable. You can't hope to avoid a battleground where expectation is met with disappointment and understanding is erroneous. It's an inevitable aspect of every journey through life, which necessarily oscillates between success and failure. There is no mountain without a valley. After a string of disappointments, some people become deeply suspicious, trusting nothing and no one and sensing deceitfulness behind everything. This is a hardening that results from a life permeated by disaster. But we can enjoy success only when we are prepared to endure defeat.

It's obvious that this self-confidence has various strengths and is relative to different contexts. No one trust themselves absolutely in every respect in every task, and no one should. But you know that you can rely on yourself. You know that you can and will act. You know that you act on your intentions, keep to plans, are capable of making agreements. You know from experience and from research that breaches of trust occur again and again, no matter how tightly you fix the wire netting. But you don't let it get you down. The firm ground that supports a life with self-confidence is therefore:

---

*"I trust, and I will sometimes be disappointed,
but I can accept that."*

This is the inner attitude that makes trust possible in a company. It's the quality of mind with which you deal with a member of staff if trust is to have any chance at all. It's that self-certainty and helpful orientation that includes awareness of the possibility of disappointment, but trusts nevertheless. It's the ability to cope with breaches of trust appropriately and impressively.

What allows self-confidence to develop? To be welcomed into the world as a child, to be loved, to be respected as a valuable person: these things build self-confidence. Experiencing success after failure also contributes to it. And for young people in their first job, it can develop when they are encouraged to think for themselves, to make decisions and to act instead of being told what to do. If we look at the results of research, the most important thing that emerges is the repeated experience of overcoming difficulties by one's own strength. *Having pulled oneself up by one's bootstraps.* The confidence that one can therefore do it again. Regaining one's confidence after failure. Having experienced oneself as capable of trust (yet again); having kept to agreements in the face of adversity. Gaining stability of action through such experiences. Working on the assumption that things will be OK, and if they go wrong, I'll manage somehow. Living with a risk because there is no reasonable alternative. And being pleased when trust is confirmed.

This applies not only to the individual but also to companies. They too need to celebrate successes: *really* celebrate them. Only then do people develop confidence that they can do even better tomorrow.

So people can be capable of trust only if they have relatively secure, prolonged contact with their own sense of reliability. Suffering can't be avoided; in fact, it is highly productive. That's why we shouldn't over-protect children, otherwise we deprive them of the opportunity to get back on their feet again. But this is an important experience that we never lose, a capacity we always carry. People know of themselves that they are capable of making agreements, that they have confidence, that they can trust themselves. Being faithful to agreements is the core of trust. Protecting ourselves necessitates keeping to agreements to preserve our self-respect. People who break trust and don't keep to agreements do themselves damage. As a rule, happiness at other people's expense doesn't work for very long.

Trust isn't just a way of looking at the world, it's a strength to deal with life. It makes it possible to cope with setbacks. Trust is an energy that never gives the future away to the opponent: it always claims it for itself. This also enhances our psychological well-being. Julian Rotter's research on interpersonal trust shows that people with a high degree of self-confidence are normally less burdened with conflict. As friends, they are held in greater esteem than their less confident peers. It's possible that their greater readiness to trust exposes them to more frequent disappointment. On the other hand, mistrustful people lose just as much by not trusting in situations where trust would be advantageous. I've never experienced anything that would refute these ideas: in reality, cautious people risk just as much as bold ones, and on top of that they forgo the thrill of boldness.

It's a weak argument: trust can lead to great benefits that are difficult or impossible to attribute directly to trust. But trust can also lead to great losses which definitely *can* be attributed to the relinquishing of control. However, loss due to mistrust can't be measured. What principle do managers follow? If they seek success, it will be trust. If they are out to avoid failure, it will be mistrust. Trust would be too risky for them, for they see only the risk, not the possible gain. What they lack is a good eye.

A good eye

Trust is inconceivable without taking a risk; it therefore requires courage. It is a bet on the future; it is located between knowing and not knowing. Under some circumstances, it entails taking risks that endanger life. But it also involves important chances.

It takes courage to reduce control, to relinquish power, to allow staff to find their own ways. It requires courage to stand up

163

for one's own values, to speak out where many remain silent: for example, when a company makes a public proclamation of trust but doesn't put it into practice. It takes courage to address the truth and not be put off by prevailing opinion. It takes courage to trust one's own intuition and judgement.

Courage is rooted in genuine self-confidence; it has to go hand in hand with respect for others. Courage has to be coupled with an interest in other people. Therefore, courage doesn't mean having no fear. Courage means *nevertheless* saying something and making oneself vulnerable. Of course, courage alone isn't sufficient, but without courage it doesn't work.

Courage is the basis for dealing with conflicts at an early stage and looking for a solution – one that doesn't make anyone into a loser. I can think of hardly any management problem that didn't result from conflicts that were avoided, allowed to drag on or dealt with inappropriately.

It's vital to distinguish courage from fearlessness. Fear helps to achieve a minimum degree of security. Some people have no fear in certain situations because other people don't mean anything to them. They may seem courageous in any conflict. And some people swing from one extreme to another, lacking any appropriateness of reaction if they encounter, say, disappointed trust.

Max Weber introduced the term *Augenmaß*: an eye for situations or a sense of proportion. This is missing if a company gears itself to maximum risk, if every snack bar takes the same precautions as a nuclear power station, if a retailer is organized like an experimental laboratory in the chemicals industry, if a bank acts as though it had to fend off a national disaster every time it grants a loan.

Management needs a sense of proportion when it comes to trust. When I argue for appropriateness, for a new measure of trust, I'm inviting you to develop new powers of judgement. Consider Dürer's knight who takes a path between the devil and death, who has replaced his pre-modern trust programme with a courageous decision that says: "I'll come through, and if I don't dare, I'll never know," who like Kierkegaard knows "fear like the dizzy feeling of freedom," who is courageous but avoids arrogance.

When I say that management needs a good eye, I say it from plenty of experience. So often I've seen managers react disproportionately when their trust is disappointed. A good eye means a balanced experience of reality, or rather the willingness to face the paradoxical structure of life. I know this balance doesn't exist in an ideal form, but all the same I maintain that some people are more able and willing to deal with the ambiguity of phenomena instead of simplifying them into a binary either/or. A realistic form of sincerity; a sense of proportion; a sense of estimation – that's the capability to make judgements about the relative importance of one thing or another. A judgement that says "This shouldn't be overlooked." A good eye makes it possible to distinguish something extreme from something appropriate; it enables you to weigh things up, but in particular it allows you to distinguish trust zones from areas of mistrust. "Do you see the battle against dishonesty and disloyalty?" "I see demotivated people and slow company processes." Management would be well advised to put their efforts into addressing the latter.

Trusting after trust has been broken

Trust is always on trial, and the trial isn't always successful. The health insurer that uses the slogan "I trust XY Health Insurance" together with a picture of a bride and groom will be aware that marriages now last about seven years on average. As the actress Hannelore Elsner put it: "I believe in love and being faithful for ever. It's just that 'for ever' is becoming a shorter and shorter period." In reality, trust is a fragile entity that you have to work on again and again. And you can be more or less successful, and setbacks can occur. The trust you've achieved may disappear. With your vulnerability you can create the conditions that facilitate trust. But you can't force the other person to trust you. That's why people skip work, work to rule and betray company secrets. That's why there is balance sheet fraud and price-rigging. That's why breaches of trust fill the gossip columns. A short war makes better headlines than a long peace... The only people who find this outrageous are the ones who believe that trust comes without a price. That is and remains a fantasy. So what if the trial isn't successful? What if trust has been destroyed? How do you deal with broken trust? Specifically, *how do you sanction a breach of trust*?

This question is of prime importance in building a trusting relationship. This is because whether an agreement is adhered to, a rule followed or a regulation taken seriously depends not least on the answer to the question "And if not, what then?"

For this purpose, we must restrict the breach of trust: if someone isn't *willing* to perform, that is undoubtedly a breach of trust. But if they are *unable* to, that isn't a breach of trust. Trust is frequently confused with expectation. However, someone who disappoints our expectations hasn't abused our trust, especially if we have excessive expectations and then find they haven't lived up to the ideal, that they are not the person we wanted them to be. "You've disappointed me" is not the same as "You've abused my trust." A breach of trust occurs only if the other person fails to adhere to agreements in which expectations are balanced. Someone likewise breaks trust if they don't adhere to agreements without having made the attempt to renegotiate. So the best way I can put it is to repeat myself: breach of trust is breach of the implicit contract.

Many people react quickly when there is a breach of trust, radiating suspicion from their squinting countenances. And we tend to look at our own behaviour through rose-tinted spectacles while prematurely assuming the other person is guilty of resentment, negligence, bad intentions and who knows what else. If we see no signs of unreliability or dishonesty, we react (often too quickly and strongly) with distrust. But not every misunderstanding is a breach of trust. We should at least ask ourselves: "What is my own part in the breach of trust? Am I shifting blame that really belongs to me? What could I have done differently?"

In relation to an individual person, mistrust may be justified, but to generalize this mistrust, as often happens like a reflex in companies, is unintelligent and counterproductive. Our habit of building up the smallest observations into anthropological archetypes, of labelling and stereotyping, is a manifestation of the same tendency. You'll often hear people saying "Typical of an engineer" or "Salesmen are always like that."

It's often not a case of concrete mistrust but merely the possibility of a breach of trust. It's often commotion, situations where there may be surprises, risks that aren't some evil phenomenon but statistical quirks. Even in the case of panic selling on the stock exchange, people talk about a crisis of confidence. This is a psychological phenomenon that's hardly based on economic fact. It's based on fantasy, the writing on the wall.

Many managers react with suspicion to the mere possibility of dishonesty. Security protection no longer begins when dangers have proved to be real, but with combating the possibility. No longer is it only the person who is believed to have done something who is under suspicion; anyone who might be guilty of abusing trust is suspected, which means everyone. Security systems are put in place as a precaution because a statistical possibility is interpreted as a probability. People want protection and prevention. You never know. Suspected dangers, worries and risks constitute full justification. Every employee has the right to protective custody.

This attitude is supported by managers' fondness for the child-rearing analogy for staff management. No doubt the fact that children are treated as a group and not primarily as individuals is helpful for this purpose. Trustworthiness isn't examined on an individual basis; thinking and decision making are carried out across the board and as a matter of principle rather than on a case-by-case basis. If one person can't be trusted, none can.

It doesn't help much to be reminded that every person is unique. Heraclitus told his pupils to "expect the unexpected." A few centuries later, Elle Woods gave similar advice in *Legally Blonde*. "You should show people more trust. You might be surprised" was the advice she gave her friend (in vain, as it turned out). The fact is that when we go looking for the worst, we'll probably find it.

Our experience of breaches of trust needn't end in generalized mistrust. Specific justified doubts are another matter. We must take into account the individual case, weigh it, keep things in proportion, even question the goal of security itself if the price to be paid for it is too high. What does this mean in practice?

Trust as the rule, mistrust as the exception, not vice versa.

Why don't people follow this simple recommendation? Here we encounter an extremely important *psychological displacement* that unfortunately this book will do little to change. Confirmed and abused trust are perceived in very different ways. The gain from confirmed trust remains invisible and isn't even detected, whereas the loss from abused trust is visible and experienced directly. Trust that's confirmed a thousand times – valuables that aren't stolen, expectations that aren't disappointed – doesn't attract further attention. It's categorised as self-evident and thus of no consequence. The many successful incidences of co-operation, the immeasurable gains from action based on trust, are noted tacitly; they don't merit comment. They are too visible to be remarkable. A single breach of trust, on the other hand, is an intense experience. It stimulates action; it gets a reaction; it gives rise immediately to consequences.

Here we have a flagrant discrepancy in perceptions of trust and the behaviour resulting from it. Company relations keep declining as guidelines intended to prevent 5 percent of people from doing what 95 percent would never do proliferate. This means that 95 percent of people have their freedom of movement curtailed because 5 percent might abuse it. Is this appropriate? Is it proportionate? Is it rational? Whatever you decide, the bad news is that you'll never catch the 5 percent. They'll always slip through your fingers. The rules of the game tell us that it's impossible to eliminate this 5 percent of blanks from the system.

But obviously it's not a question of doing something that makes economic sense, weighing opportunities and risks, comparing the cost of regulation with the gain in security. No, it's above all a question of being able to justify oneself. You've done everything humanly possible, but if something still happens, well, there's nothing you can do, so management can wash its hands of the problem. Who cares whether it makes economic sense? In any case, economic logic takes second place to the compulsion to justify oneself.

Let's avoid any misunderstanding here. It may be that rules, indeed extremely strict rules, must prevail the greater the actual threat of potential harm. We aren't permitted to escape the bounds of logical self-preservation. In terms of a company that wishes to increase its returns on trust, these rules can, however, only be the last resort. We must always consider the scale and the price to be paid for the loss of trust-based interaction. Many companies' mania for regulation defies this principle. It's absurd that any act that isn't expressly permitted should be prohibited for the sake of self-protection.

But how can we react specifically and sensibly to an individual breach of trust if we don't wish to be separated immediately from our colleagues? There's a preconception that persists stubbornly, especially among Germans, that companies are held together by the harmonious interplay and understanding of employees. Only very rarely does it become clear that it is in fact the handling of conflicts that provides the real social cement in our companies. In order for trust to average more gains than losses, evolution has developed a highly successful strategy that goes by the name of "tit for tat." This was first discovered by game theorists working on the Prisoner's Dilemma, and then applied to evolutionary research: look, it's clearly at work even at the level of bacteria. It can be found, as A. K. Treml proved, at every level of life. Accordingly, under no circumstances does trust require altruistic motivation for behaviour (we can hardly expect that of bacteria), but simply the possibility of winning the game.

Tit for tat always starts by offering another player (think of one of your colleagues here) co-operation and trust. If they confirm this trust, then you in turn reply to their behaviour with trust. This way, greater benefit can be achieved *together* than if one player makes gains at the expense of someone else. If the other suddenly behaves uncooperatively, if they abuse the trust placed in them to their sole advantage, then you react immediately as the disappointed player by withdrawing co-operation. You put a stop to communication. You withdraw your trust from them, in full knowledge of what you are doing. But only temporarily. After an appropriate period, after another round of the game, you offer them trust again. You thus give them the opportunity to reward your trust again and at the same time to repair their earlier breach of trust. They have a chance to learn from their mistakes. You offer them this trust only one more time, though, not a third time. Frank, clear confrontation creates trust, becomes predictable. Preconceptions of perfect harmony, truces and missed opportunities for sanctions can only generate new mistrust.

This is *second-chance ethics*. Its rules are:

1. Always offer to co-operate first.
2. If your offer is returned, be prepared to trust in the long term; if not, then punish immediately and mercilessly.
3. Offer trust again after a certain period.

A second chance may be valued even more highly than the first, though this varies from culture to culture. In the United States, entrepreneurs who have already gone bankrupt once have much better chances with banks and new employers. Having experienced failure, they are regarded as more worthy of trust than people who haven't yet stood with their career in ruins at their feet.

As a successful example of second-chance ethics, I'd like to cite the woman who, in addition to her career, also cooked for her three men: her husband and two adult sons. The agreement was "I'll cook for you, but you clean up the kitchen afterwards. It's up to you how you organize that among yourselves." For a time, this worked well. Then the men started not to take their *quid pro quo* quite so seriously. The woman noticed the neglect, made it clear she wasn't happy with it, and, when the men didn't change, took action: she stopped cooking. Imagine the shock: they'd expected nagging or angry scenes, but not *action*. For a few days domestic bliss was in short supply; they survived on takeaways and the like. Then the woman began to cook again. Her men gratefully accepted the offer, pleased to be given another chance. Since then they have stuck rigidly to the agreement – to this day, to the best of my knowledge.

From this example you can deduce that:

A breach of trust is not evidence for the non-existence of a mechanism of trust.

"Punish immediately and mercilessly" may seem to you a hostile reaction, not one that fits the self-image of the generous sovereign. But it works. If trust is important to you, you should consciously accept the price to be paid in order to discipline uncooperative players. If you aren't prepared to pay the price, then trust isn't important to you. Under no circumstances, however, should you turn a blind eye. Don't allow someone to break your implicit trust. If you don't act, you are an accomplice, as good as saying "It's OK to abuse trust." Many people like nothing more than the magnanimity of being understanding or, worse, forgiving. If you want to exploit the other's feelings of guilt, you will in fact do it most successfully by showing understanding, by forgiving. But if you want to restore a symmetrical relationship, an eye-to-eye partnership that facilitates action based on trust, then you should dispense with patronising condescension. The only thing that works is a price to be paid. The other person must, at least for a time, pay for their breach of trust. Only then can things get back to an even keel.

It's often said that trust can't flourish in a climate of fear. This is wrong. The reverse is true: if we can't trust the police to do their job, trust that the rules of the game will be enforced, then there is no framework for reliable co-operation. A company functions only if its members adhere to agreements. If they don't, there must be sanctions for the breach of agreement. Without sanctions there would never be clear co-operation agreements. It is not fear that destabilizes trust, but the absence of fear.

We must react quickly to a breach of trust, otherwise it may be taken as the norm, or indeed become the rule. After a Serb murdered the heir to the Austro-Hungarian empire on 28 June 1914, it took four weeks for Austria-Hungary to issue an ultimatum to Serbia. As the weeks had gone by, public opinion around the world had assumed that the attack would be swallowed without consequence. When Austria-Hungary then retaliated, its actions weren't really understood. A similar thing happened in the merger between Daimler and Chrysler. The people at Daimler feared they might look like know-it-all German invaders in the United States, so they delayed stepping in at Chrysler. Their hesitation made their late intervention seem authoritarian, tactless and typically German.

For management this means react quickly. Whether it be immediately or after sleeping on it depends on the situation. But don't wait too long. It's inappropriate and incomprehensible to employees if you wait for the final straw and then restrict an employee's freedom to elbow room only.

Tit for tat also applies in the event of *you* doing something wrong. Don't cover it up, but face up to it fairly and squarely. "My behaviour wasn't acceptable, and that matters to me. Will you give me another chance?" Scarcely anyone would deny you. The tit for tat strategy developed by Anatole Rapoport is impressive proof of the premise tested in the computer tournaments initiated by Robert Axelrod: that the gains in co-operation achievable in the long term under conditions of trust are greater than those under mistrust.

Maturana tells a story in this vein about students in halls of residence. A young Asian man was the butt of many jokes and tricks from the others. Nowadays it would probably be called bullying. They did everything they could to make life difficult for him. One day they confessed and told him they wouldn't play any more tricks on him from now on. He could hardly believe it. "You mean you won't tie my shirts in knots any more, or put dead mice in my bed?" "No," they said. "We won't do things like that any more." "OK," he said, "Then I won't piss in your coffee any more."

The tit for tat strategy appeals to us. You should always start co-operation with a co-operative effort. It's pragmatic to face the world with moderate trust, assuming that people usually have good intentions and mean well until we have reason to suspect otherwise. This may be moral, but above all it is self-interested. Under no circumstances should we take the moral high ground. Trust arising from self-interest is a far more powerful strategy. Most educational attempts to instil altruistic motivations for action have been ineffective. Self-interest based on short-term advantage is stupid. The clever egotist co-operates, so a revolutionary admonition would be "Put your interests first: co-operate!"

We encounter this in everyday life: the baker isn't friendly to us just because she likes us, but because she wants us to come again. If she was unfriendly several times, we'd go to the competition. And the tit for tat rule can, in turn, give rise to the exciting hope that, in an increasingly global society, behaviour that breaks trust will decline; not just because suddenly everyone starts to love their neighbour, but because they have to bear in mind that at some time or another they may come into contact again. Even today it's true to say that "What goes around, comes around," so the initial investment in trust is worth while.

Can trust also be restored in this way? Yes, albeit very slowly. One company made great efforts under a new managing director to create an atmosphere of openness after a long patriarchal tradition of mistrust. The company decided to make an annual budget of around 5,000 euros freely available to every sales executive for marketing purposes, and told them they needn't produce any documentation to account for the money. Shortly before the year end, the accounts were checked for debits. Not a single euro had been withdrawn. In this case, a second chance was needed to conquer the mistrust.

Confidence in trust

Following the rules of co-operation makes sense only if I am able to assume that the other party is following them too. Otherwise I am the one being played for a fool. This is precisely what many fear: they are convinced that others' co-operation is lacking and they themselves will look stupid. They have no confidence in the trust of others. They say "I don't have a problem with trust, but I'm not so sure whether I can trust others" or, more tellingly, "I wouldn't have a problem with trust." And because everyone thinks like this, nothing happens. The demonstrably inaccurate yet widely held assumption about everyone else's readiness to deceive prevents the atmosphere of trust that virtually everyone prefers from actually developing. People are locked into a world where trust is halved, so to speak.

We tend to overestimate our own trustworthiness and underestimate others'. Lies, differences of opinion and disappointed expectations are lumped together, along with lack of dependability and cultural differences, and there you have it: "You simply can't trust anyone!" Then the downward spiral commences, and each suspects the other of copying their own good intentions. What Martin Heidegger describes for people can also apply to companies: "Togetherness in people is absolutely not an isolated, indifferent juxtaposition, but an exciting, ambiguous looking-out for each other, a secret listening to each other. A conflict is being played out behind the mask of unity."

Above all, "confidence in trust" (Tanja Ripperger), confidence in the willingness of others to trust, is a necessity on the road to a culture of trust that is worthy of the name. Every player, irrespective of whether they are boss, colleague or employee, simultaneously places trust in and is trusted by the other. They dispense with explicit safety precautions by trusting in the fact that the other also trusts and is aware that they have this in common. That is confidence in the functioning and general recognition of the trust mechanism in the company. It derives its creative force from the collective advantageousness of trust. For example, a department makes resources available while trusting that if it needed resources it would receive them from another department. This trust is based on the expectation that the participants are aware that they have trust in common. It works in orchestras, churches, hospitals and partnerships, frequently despite a very great strain on trust.

But this trust can't be scheduled. This is why it's so unwieldy for traditional management. If there is insufficient courage to make oneself vulnerable, trust can develop only very slowly through interaction and the building of relationships, and blossom only when frequently put to the test. This is countered by the familiar speedy erosion of trust: a single disappointment is often all it takes to shake trust for a long time. Also important for companies is the "halo effect" or shockwaves from an incident. Trust-destroying behaviour leaves its epicentre and radiates throughout the entire organization.

The development and continuation of a culture of trust essentially depend on how many others also use the trust mechanism. Like knowledge, trust is a resource that changes with use. It atrophies when unused and grows stronger with frequent use. The more trust is used, the more it is generated, as it were. So trust isn't just a matter of balance, but also of turnover, of give and take. Low turnover generates low profits. High turnover generates high profits. It creates wealth.

Profound trust doesn't just drop into our laps; it has to be earned. It isn't a resource that exhausts itself, but one that increases with use. A critical mass of players, especially at management level, is exceedingly helpful: these are the seeds that, when they germinate, can develop into a culture of trust. They must have access to that courage that is nourished by self-esteem if management is to be willing and able to trust in spite of everything; to offer trust up front, in the clear knowledge that they may be disappointed. This also applies to appointing staff:

---

*A trusting management is surrounded
by trusting employees.*

The readiness of an individual to trust and to honour trust, however, is in turn fundamentally determined by the company's institutional framework. Is trust experienced as a social norm, or

177

just claimed? How detailed or vague are contracts? How many rules and regulations are there? Above all, is trust a worthwhile strategy, or is it in fact penalized?

If trust is important to you, then you should get together with your colleagues and answer the following questions:

- What do we as a management team do to promote trust in our company?
- What are the criteria, behaviour and data we can use to identify a culture of trust?
- What and where are the critical trust-related issues?
- What are the biggest hurdles to building trust in our company?
- Which of our rules are contrary to trust?
- What do we do as a management team to promote trust among ourselves?

Trust isn't a matter of models and mission statements. The acid test is *the concrete behaviour of the person fixing the values in cases of conflict.* This attitude determines whether an atmosphere of trust can develop. This person setting the standard for the company is surely the CEO, chairman of the board, managing director or proprietor. The person setting the standard for *your* area of responsibility, though, is *you*, because a culture of trust exists only incompletely if at all. It's a microcosmic phenomenon between you and your colleagues, between this person and that; how you behave not when everything's right with the world, but when the going gets tough. Generally speaking, people will react as sensitively as a seismograph to your specific behaviour in difficult situations, and that's the rule of the game by which all are guided.

Take mistakes, for example. Do you react proactively, or do you complain? What about critical feedback? Are you grateful for frankness, or do you respond by justifying yourself? Do you even go on the offensive? Only the mean-spirited find dissent invigorating. Do you place your trust in others up front? How much? Do you really make yourself vulnerable? Do you tackle every structural problem with a directive? Do your employees feel encouraged to express differing opinions? Do you respect others' views? Do you find them valuable? Do you seek input from your employees? Which people do you promote? The mistrustful or the trusting? The yes-men or the independent thinkers?

But above all, and the power of this seems particularly important to me, you must honour age for its age, otherwise the consensus of trust crumbles. It's not just that I've become increasingly doubtful whether the career-orientated window-dressing of young MBA job-hoppers is in line with company survival. For millennia it was the elders who were entrusted with leadership duties. We have sound anthropological reasons for this. Many executives rise far too quickly, and many older managers leave far too soon.

As a manager, you must consider the effect on trust of any action by management. In addition, you can create contexts that facilitate the birth and spread of trust within the company. Remove all counterproductive structures. Weaken internal disputes. Strengthen not only togetherness, but also support. Show that you trust your employees, operate on the premise that they have a personal right to quality at work, not just one that is imposed, and demonstrate that they can organize themselves to a great extent, that they can manage their time themselves. Give people responsibility. They must feel "It's all down to me. I may be replaceable, but then an important link would be missing. And if I fail, then it becomes a problem for my boss and everyone else. I make a difference. And that difference is needed here." If you trust, it means not planning to safeguard yourself against each and every eventuality over long periods. It means dealing with disruption locally, immediately and at a low level, instead of warding off every occurrence, banishing all doubt. Otherwise how would there be innovation? Trusting other people encourages them to trust us. If we distrust others, they start to distrust us. So put your cards on the table. Be honest. Even if you feel distrust.

Every manager, you *personally*, can make a bit more effort to trust in your personal environment. You can also disassociate yourself in your immediate sphere of influence from the distrustful attitudes of head office and supervisory authorities. Many responsible managers act in their company's best interest by *not* strictly adhering to unhelpful policies made by top-level management. They form pockets of resistance that are enclaves of reciprocal vulnerability in the face of barrages of distrust. Their efforts are all the more remarkable when one considers the limitations within which they work.

One last time: "Trust is good, control is better." This phrase forms the basis of many people's view of life. A company that focuses on challenging its employees' creative forces is more likely to quote Freiherr vom Stein: "Trust honours the man, eternal guardianship prevents him maturing." What is the role of a trusting economic organization? To organize a company that frees people from depending on instructions by opening up opportunities for development. To create space for common entrepreneurial action: that's the goal. This is in keeping with some companies' efforts to invest in employees' lifelong employability as a social security measure.

What this all means for co-operation is:

If you work with someone, you should trust them.
If you don't trust them, you would do better not to work
with them.

There is no third way. You can't perfect anti-escape systems to the extent that you have no need to fear permanent deception. This trust isn't blind, but is given up front until the opposite is proven.

The more complex the environment, the greater the reciprocal effect of decisions and actions within the company, and the greater the need for confidence in trust. The mechanism of trust not only reduces the cost of working together but initially facilitates co-operation, which wouldn't exist at all without trust, or only at a prohibitively high price. Trust therefore creates social capital within the company. This social capital largely consists of an internalized standard of trust and a corresponding conscience. An organization imbued with trust will thus have long-term competitive advantages. These advantages will increase with the level of insecurity and frequency of co-operation the longer they last and the less hierarchical control is possible. Companies that succeed in building a culture of trust are able to maximize achievable co-operation profits and reduce transaction costs. The investment in trust pays for itself.

Companies characterized by mistrust aren't able to change as quickly and comprehensively as the market. Consequently, companies everywhere are faced with the need to grant parts of themselves greater autonomy as market events accelerate. If they succeed in expanding these necessarily incomplete contracts by means of the mechanism of trust and manage to make them productive, these companies are successful in the marketplace. Indeed, it is through modern organizational forms such as virtual companies or networks whose success is based on multiplying their own resources through spatially and temporally remote co-operation that trust will increase in importance as an organizational principle.

A model of trust

We have now reached a point from which we can look back on the most important elements of the trust process. This diagram condenses them into a model:

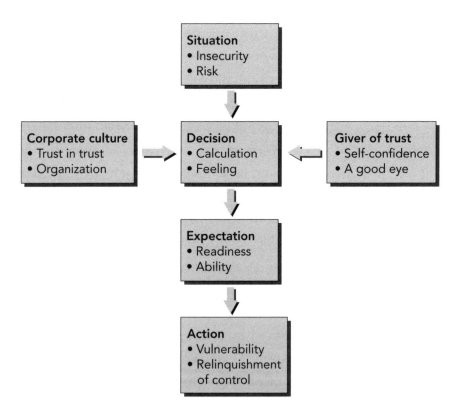

Reading from top to bottom: the need for trust increases only in an insecure and risky situation. The decision to trust is then the result of rational calculation mixed with emotional processes. This decision requires self-confidence on the part of the trust giver, and a good eye. To these are added corporate culture factors that include a generally shared confidence in trust. If a player, perhaps you as manager, decides to place their trust in someone, then they expect the employee to be capable of making an effort and ready to do so, or at least not to harm them. You are translating your decision to trust into action, you are waiving control and you are thus making yourself vulnerable.

The right to trust

But under real conditions in a company, is it actually possible to manage by trusting? Time and again I hear the objection, "No one is interested in candour and reliability." The situation isn't encouraging. Indeed, in big conglomerates office politics often suppress any burgeoning honesty. Theodor W. Adorno once said "There is no true life in lies." Applied to corporate relations, this means that when subjected to force, even the most well-meaning gesture is suspected of being an attempt at manipulation. And that's precisely what they intend. There's nothing wrong with manipulation unless one pretends not to intend to manipulate. If I announce my manipulative intent ("I want you to prove yourself trustworthy"), then I can see nothing immoral in it, since trust doesn't mean a lack of intent (M. Göpel). The fact that I have a relationship of trust with someone in no way precludes me wanting them to carry out a specific action. Whether in so doing my intent destroys the trust doesn't depend on *whether* I have an intention, but on *what* my intention is.

If I regard the other person as a kind of machine that I can control, then trust is not the only thing that will be destroyed. The other person will teach me otherwise by making use of their freedom. If on the other hand I grant the other person freedom and self-determination, then the conditions for the development of trust are favourable. How they behave ultimately, whether they exploit my co-operative behaviour or not, whether they exploit my vulnerability or not, is their decision, a decision that contains an unavoidable moment of freedom. Since it isn't possible to circumvent the other's freedom, the wise person utilizes it: not by generating resistance but by allowing freedom to be productive en route to my goal. In this case my behaviour is directed not towards *restricting* the other's freedom, but towards expanding it; not limiting their opportunities for choice and action, but increasing them.

The key to a culture of trust is consequently the attitude – not just pretended but felt deep within – that each individual matters, that their personal interests and needs count, so that they are self-determining individuals. No management method will ever work if it is lacking in genuine respect for the individual. In relationships of trust, the participants have a reciprocal influence on each other. The dynamic is circular, as we have seen. They grow together. The trick is to decide to trust even though we doubt, even though we are unsure. This *decision to trust* is the first and most important step towards becoming a more trusting person. If we don't take this step, nothing happens, so we must combat the fear and cynicism inside us, we must look at the world through different eyes, because ultimately trust, like so much else, is in the eye of the beholder. When you ask "How do I earn the trust of others?" the only answer can be "Be trustworthy yourself." Trustworthiness is one of the great secrets of a happy life – and of successful management. Trustworthy managers never see their employees just as means, but always as ends too. They always think of others. The answer lies in every one of us. The responsibility for a serious culture of trust can't be passed on to a programme, or delegated to a tool. It depends on our readiness to play a part in the mechanism of trust. To make ourselves vulnerable.

The golden rule:

Every employee has a right to trust.

Every employee has a right to be recognized as a trustworthy person. This attitude doesn't suddenly dissipate the tension between trust and distrust, but it does turn it around such that trust might conceivably become the company's lifeblood. Of course, trust is a risky business, but the risk of not trusting is greater.

The forces of mistrust are stronger than ever, but they aren't invincible. Many managers are tired of providing the level of reassurance associated with mistrust. Instead of *managing* mistrust, we should use our energies to *overcome* it. To do this, we need to develop a new power to discern trust: a reasonable and persuasive position between excess and understatement. This is a job for individuals, because the state of equilibrium is always remote from the standard, from the norm, from centralized regulation. Because it can only be achieved on the spot, on a case-by-case basis, in the knowledge of the precise circumstances, it must to a great extent remain an individual decision. How else can an individual be explained if not by their power to reach a considered decision, which alone allows proportion? The perceptive spirit, the decisive intent, perhaps incorporating feelings, can't be subjected to toeing the line to order. Time and again, the central authorities should strengthen their management forces on the ground, not hamstring them. The company must put itself in the hands of its managers; if not them, then whom? The centralist hope that only rules and quantifiable mechanical procedures might prevail is for ever unattainable. We must develop into individual bastions of consideration, personally balancing trust and mistrust, taking into account the current concrete facts of the matter. We must switch from a culture of standardization to one of success. Only then will a company become (or perhaps I should say return to being) a flexible, fast, economically fit entity for the future.

A company based on trust. Inconceivable? Maybe. But not working towards it is proof of irresponsible faintness of heart. It's high time, and it's not yet too late.

An historical afterword

Rousseau said that foresight is the true source of all our suffering. Because security is an illusion; an individual and social *fata morgana*. Life is always life-threatening. If we don't trust, we live in constant fear. Living your life in fear is worse by far than occasionally being deceived. Then we are living in a situation that we ourselves have created. If we watch others fearfully, ultimately we are watching ourselves, because the walls that we build for others surround us. That which is intended to shut out others imprisons us. The price of the illusion of protection is restricted freedom of movement. It lets us do little more than crawl through life.

But thank goodness genetic varieties don't work in concert with mistrust. Because trust isn't only effective, cost-cutting and quick, it's also simply gratifying. It lets us blossom. It's fun living and working in a climate of trust. That's why, irrespective of economic considerations, the question always inescapably facing us is

"Under what conditions do we want to live?" No one can force us to lead a life steeped in mistrust. Even after a breach of trust we always have the choice. We mustn't barricade ourselves into safety containers, we mustn't allow a life of fighting for survival to be forced on us, we mustn't encumber our lives with fearful watchfulness. Even under the most unrewarding conditions, the same rule still applies: the decision is always yours.

The former head of Bosch, Hans Merkle, addressed the concept of trust in great depth in his memoirs *The Stony Road*. In his opinion, Julius Caesar epitomizes a life of trust lived out under difficult conditions. Caesar knew for years that he would be murdered. Powerful forces consider him and his dictatorial power to be the death-knell of the *res publica*. They hold him responsible for the decline of everything that made Rome proud. But Caesar doesn't protect himself. He doesn't carry weapons, he walks through the streets without a bodyguard, he dispenses with guards outside his house. From time to time, he is beset by fear and doubt. But he still disdains protection.

His friends accuse him of lack of care. Shakespeare has his wife Calpurnia warn him: "Alas! my lord, your wisdom is consum'd in confidence; do not go forth to-day" on the very day on which he is murdered. As far as we know, Caesar was not only aware for years of the constant danger in which he lived – "If I were not Caesar, I would be Caesar's murderer" (Thornton Wilder) – he was even deeply initiated in the plans of those who sought his blood. He knew the perpetrators, time and place of his murder before it took place. And yet he still goes to the Capitol, delivers himself up, stares danger in the face. He doesn't arm himself, continues to go unguarded. And is murdered.

An irritating image, a disturbing message. Does Caesar have a death-wish? Is he facing up to a phobia, doing what he most fears?

Is his trust blind? No; quite the opposite, it seems. Caesar wishes to remain true to himself. He doesn't want to reject the significant by hanging on to the insignificant. He doesn't want to take flight and contribute to the general hothouse atmosphere of insecurity. In his mind, vulnerability is the sign of humanity. He is so full of self-esteem, so very much a leader, and so very aware of the effect of his actions that, like Socrates before him and Jesus of Nazareth after him, he shapes his death as a symbol of living virtue. He doesn't die *of* something, he dies *for* something. Trust in life in the face of impending certain death. Being unprotected even though he knows his trust is being abused.

Is that negligent? Is it naïve? No, it is a decision. It is the decision not to let mistrust have power over him. The inescapable, the ultimate paradox persists, available only to the human mind: he trusts, although he mistrusts.

BIBLIOGRAPHY

Albach, H.: "Vertrauen in der ökonimischen Theorie" [Trust in Economic Theory], in: *Zeitschrift für die gesamten Staatswissenschaften,* 1, 1990, pp. 2–11.

Anders, G.: "eBay learns to trust again," in *Fast Company,* 12, 2001, pp. 102–5.

Axelrod, R.: Die Evolution der Kooperation [The Evolution of Cooperation], Munich 1991.

Baba, M.L.: "Dangerous Liaisons: Trust, distrust and information technology in American work organizations," in: *Human Organization,* 3, 1999, pp. 331–46.

Baier, T.: "Trust and Antitrust," in: *Ethics,* 1986, pp. 231–60.

Bastian, T: "Archaisch und verdrängt: Der Affekt Scham" [Archaic and Repressed: The effect of shame] in: *Universitas,* 10, 1994, pp. 992–98.

Bastian, T. and Hilgers, M: "Kain. Die Trennung von Scham und Schuld" [Cain: The Separation of shame and guilt] in: *Psyche,* 44, pp. 1100–12.

Beckert, J., Metzner, A. and Roehl, H.: "Vertrauenserosion als organisatorische Gefahr und wie ihr zu begegnen ist" [Erosion of Trust as an Organizational Danger and How to Counter it], in: *Organisationsentwicklung* 4, 98, pp. 56–66.

Bieri, P.: *Das Handwerk der Freiheit. Über die Entdeckung des eigenen Willens* [The Craft of Freedom: On the discovery of one's own will], Munich 2001.

Bok, S.: *Lying: Moral choice in public and private life,* Pantheon Books, New York, 1978.

Breen, B.: "Trickle-Up Leadership," in *Fast Company,* 11, 2001, pp. 70–72.

Deutsch, M.: "Cooperation and Trust," in Jones, M.R. (ed.): *Nebraska Symposium on Motivation,* University of Nebraska Press, Lincoln, 1962, pp. 275–320.

Dickmann, M.: "Führung als Management von Tauschbeziehungen" [Leadership as the Management of Exchange Relationships], in: *Personalführung,* 6, 2001, pp. 84–7.

Domizlaff, H.: Markentechnik – die Gewinnung des öffentlichen Vertrauens [Brand Technique – Gaining Public Trust], Hamburg 1929.

Dyer, C.: "Interview" in: *brandeins,* 2, 2001, pp. 119–24.

Eberle, W. and Hartwich, L.: "Brennpunkt Führungspotential" [Focus on Management Potential], Frankfurt am Main 1995.

Fox, A.: *Beyond Contract: Work, power and trust relations,* Faber, London, 1974.

Gambetta, D.: "Can we trust Trust?" in: Gambetta, D. (ed.): *Trust: Making and breaking cooperative relations,* Blackwell Publishers, Oxford, 1988, pp. 213–38.

Geramanis, O.: *Vertrauen – die Entstehung einer sozialen Ressource* [Trust – The Creation of a Social Resource], Stuttgart 2002.

Gerhardt, V.: *Selbstbestimmung. Das Prinzip der Individualität* [Self-Determination: The principle of individuality], Stuttgart 1999.

Gerhardt, V.: *Individualität. Das Element der Welt* [Individuality: The element of the world], Munich 2000.

Glanville, R.: "The Man in the Train – Complexity, Unmanageability, Conversation and Trust," in: Wüthrich, H.A. et al. (ed.) in: *Grenzen ökonomischen Denkens*, Wiesbaden, 2001, pp. 311–52.

Govier, T.: *Dilemmas of Trust*, McGill-Queen's University Press, Montreal, 1998.

Granovetter, M.: "The Strength of Weak Ties," in: *American Journal of Sociology*, 78, 1973, pp. 1360–80.

Guehenno, J.-M., *The End of the Nation-State*, Minneapolis, University of Minnesota Press, 1995.

Hahne, A.: *Kommunikation in der Organisation. Grundlagen und Analyse* [Communication in the Organization: Principles and analysis], Opladen 1997.

Handy, C.: "Trust and the Virtual Organization," in: *Harvard Business Review*, 5/6, 1995, pp. 41–50.

Heimburg, Y. v.: "Führung in virtuellen Teams" [Management in Virtual Teams], in: *Personalführung*, 2, 2002, pp. 1–3.

Heuser, U.J.: "Unruhe als Prinzip" [Unrest as a Principle], in: *Die Zeit*, No. 6, 03.02.2000, p. 22.

Hoff, A.: *Vertrauensarbeitszeit: einfach flexibel arbeiten* [Time to Work with Trust: Just Work Flexibly], Wiesbaden 2002.

James, G.: Digitale Elite [Digital Elite], Sankt Gallen 1997.

Kieler, T., Müller, W.H. and Eicken, S.: "Befindlichkeit in der chemischen Industrie" [Sensitivities in the Chemical Industry], in: *WWZ Forum 59*, Basel 2001.

Kittel, R.: "Vertrauen aus dem Glas" [Trust in a Jar], in: *GDI Impuls*, 1, 2002, pp.24–31.

Kouzes, J.M. and Posner, B.Z.: *Credibility: How leaders gain and lose it, why people demand it*, Jossey-Bass Wiley, San Francisco, 1993.

Kramer, R.M. and Tyler, T.R.: *Trust in Organizations*, Sage Publications, New York, 1996.

Kramer, R.M.: "Trust and Distrust in Organizations," in: *Annual Review of Psychology*, 50, 1999, pp. 569–98.

Krell, G.: "Vertrauensorganisation als Antwort auf Wertewechesl und Technologieschub?" [Organization of Trust as a Response to Changing Values and the Advance of Technology], in: *Zeitschrift für Organisationsentwicklung*, 2, 1991, pp. 35–50.

Lamparter, D.H.: "Kulturrevolution auf schwäbische Art" [A Swabian-style Cultural Revolution], in: *Die Zeit*, No. 36, 30.08.2001, p.17.

Leadbeater, C.: *Living on Thin Air: The new economy*, Penguin, New York, 2000.

Levering, R. and Moskowitz, M.: "The 100 best companies to work for in America," in: *Fortune*, 1, 2000, pp. 82–110.

Littman, P. and Jansen, St. A.: *Oszillator. Virtualisierung – die permanente Neuerfindung der Organisation* [Oscillator. Virtualization – the Continual Reinvention of the Organization], Stuttgart 2000.

Luhmann, N.: *Vertrauen. Ein Mechanismus der Reduktion sozialer Komplexität* [Trust: A mechanism for the reduction of social complexity], 3rd edition, Stuttgart 1989.

Malik, F.: "Das Management des Kopfarbeiters" [Management of Brainworkers], in: *News-Spezial*, 3, 2001, pp. 74–5.

Malik, F.: *Führen, Leisten, Leben* [Managing, Performing, Living], Munich 2001.

Maxwell, J.C.: *The 21 Irrefutable Laws of Leadership*, Nelson Thornes, Nashville, 1998.

McLean Parks, J.: "The Contracts of Individuals and Organizations," in: *Research in Organizational Behavior*, 15, 1993, pp. 1–40.

Müller, W.R.: "Welche Welten sollen gelten, oder: Was ist der Mitarbeiter wert?" [Which Worlds are Valid, or: What is an Employee Worth?], in: Bruhn. M. et al. (eds.): *Wertorientierte Unternehmerführung* [Value-oriented Company Management], Wiesbaden 1998.

Oelsnitz, D.v.d.: "Walt Disney – ein Lehrstück in Sachen Management" [Walt Disney – an Example in Management Matters], in: *Frankfurter Allgemeine Zeitung*, 281, 03.12.2001, p. 28.

Orthey, F.M.: "Dressur der Befreiung. Management zwischen großen Zwängen und kleinen Freiheiten" [Conditioning for Liberation: Management between major pressures and minor freedoms], in: *Universitas*, 643, 1, 2000, pp. 54-66.

Preisendörfer, P.: "Vertrauen als Soziologische Kategorie" [Trust as a Sociological Category], in: *Zeitschrift für Soziologie* 24, 1995, pp. 263–72.

Pothast, U.: *Lebendige Vernünftigkeit* [Living Reasonableness], Frankfurt am Main 1998.

Priddat, B.P.: "Zukunft der Arbeit" [The Future of Work], in: *Universitas* 2, 1999, pp. 133–41.

Ripperger, T.: *Ökonomik des Vertrauens* [The Economy of Trust], Tübingen 1998.

Risch, S.: "Eine feine Gesellschaft" [A Fine Society], in: *managermagazin*, 4, 1999, pp. 255–75.

Reina, D.S. and Reina, M.L.: *Trust & Betrayal in the Workplace*, Berrett-Koehler Publishers San Francisco, 1999.

Robinson, S.L.: "Trust and breach of the psychological contract," in: *Administrative Science Quarterly*, 41, 1996, pp. 574–99.

Rousseau, D.M.: *Psychological Contracts in Organization: Understanding written and unwritten agreements*, Sage Publications, Thousand Oaks, 1995.

Rotter, J.B.: "Interpersonal Trust, Trustworthiness, and Gullibility," in: *American Psychologist*, 35, 1980, pp. 1–7.

Rust, H.: "Kampf um die Besten" [The Battle for the Best], in: *manager-magazin*, 4, 2000, pp. 241–58.

Rust, H.: "Die Ewiggestrigen" [Yesterday's Men], in: *netmanager*, 3, 2001, p. 30.

Schäffer, U.: *Kontrolle als Lernprozess* [Supervision as a Learning Process], Wiesbaden 2001.

Scott, D.: "The Causal Relationship between Trust and the Assessed Value of Management by Objectives," in: *Journal of Management*, 2, 1980, pp. 157–75.

Seifert, M.: *Vertrauensmanagement im Unternehmen* [Trust Management in Companies], Munich 2001.

Sen, A.K.: "Goals, Commitment and Identity," in: *Journal of Law, Economics and Organisation*, 1, 1985, pp. 341–55.

Staudt, E.: "Mobilität ist eine Illusion" [Mobility is an Illusion], in: *Welt am Sonntag* 42, 21.10.2001.

Sydow, J. "Virtuelle Unternehmung – Erfolg als Vertrauensorganisation" [Virtual Enterprise – Success as an Organization of Trust], in: *Office Management* 7–8/1996, p. 13.

Treml, A.K.: "Zufall, Schlamperei und Sex" [Chance, Sloppiness and Sex], in: *Universitas* 2000, pp. 562–71.

Ulrich, A.: "Vertrauen oder Wissenschaft" [Trust or Science], in: *eigentümlich frei*, 17, 2001, p. 34.

Walzer, M.: "Mut, Mitleid und ein gutes Auge" [Courage, Compassion and a Good Eye], in: *Deutsche Zeitschrift für Philosophie*, 48, 2000), pp. 709–718.

Werner, G.W.: Das Füreinander Leisten. Wirtschaft als Kultur-Übung" [Performing for One Another. Economics as a Cultural Exercise], in: *gdi-Impuls*, 50, 2000, pp. 46–50.

Werner, J.: "Vertrauen" [Trust], in: *Wirtschaftswoche*, 11, 2000, p. 62.

Zand, D.E.: *Wissen, Führen, Überzeugen* [Knowing, Leading, Convincing], Heidelberg 1983.